SECRET
RENO

A Guide to the Weird, Wonderful, and Obscure

Janice Oberding

Copyright © 2021, Reedy Press, LLC
All rights reserved.

Reedy Press
PO Box 5131
St. Louis, MO 63139
www.reedypress.com

No part of this publication may be reproduced or transmitted in any form or by any means, electronic or mechanical, including photocopy, recording, or any information storage and retrieval system, without permission in writing from the publisher. Permissions may be sought directly from Reedy Press at the above mailing address or via our website at www.reedypress.com.

Library of Congress Control Number: 2020950055
ISBN: 9781681063072

Design by Jill Halpin

Cover images: Poker chips, bowling stadium, last chance Joe, and author headshot by Bill Oberding; camel rider courtesy of the Virginia City Tourism Commission.

Unless otherwise indicated, all interior photos are by Bill Oberding.

We (the publisher and the author) have done our best to provide the most accurate information available when this book was completed. However, we make no warranty, guarantee, or promise about the accuracy, completeness, or currency of the information provided, and we expressly disclaim all warranties, express or implied. Please note that attractions, company names, addresses, websites, and phone numbers are subject to change or closure, and this is outside of our control. We are not responsible for any loss, damage, injury, or inconvenience that may occur due to the use of this book. When exploring new destinations, please do your homework before you go. You are responsible for your own safety and health when using this book.

Printed in the United States of America
21 22 23 24 25   5 4 3 2 1

In loving memory of Terri Hall-Peltier,
a Renoite who knew and loved her city and its people.

CONTENTS

ix .... Acknowledgments

1 .... Introduction

2 .... A Little Rivalry

4 .... General Jesse L. Reno Statue

6 .... Kiss the Courthouse Pillar

8 .... Wedding Ring Bridge Legend

10 .... The Biggest Little City in the World

12 .... The Blarney Stone . . . a Piece of It Anyway

14 .... World's Tallest Artificial Climbing Wall

16 .... Lazy Days on the Truckee

18 .... Jeans

20 .... The Donner Party Camped Here

22 .... Windy Hill (Audrey Harris Park)

24 .... The Gazebo at Huffaker Moutain

26 .... Wa-Pai-Shone at Rose Garden Idlewild Park

28 .... National Bowling Stadium, International Bowling Museum & Hall of Fame (Reno Satellite)

30 .... The Lear Theater

32 .... Artown

34 .... Virginia Lake

36 .... Giant Poker Chips

38 .... Miss Wakayama and the Two-Headed Calf

40 .... Giddy Up

42 .... Reno Rodeo

44 .... An Elephant Named Bertha

46 .... Divorces and Dude Ranches

48 .... Dymaxion Car

Page	Title
50	The Mansion That Moved Twice
52	Reno's Greatest Unsolved Mystery
54	Marilyn's Last Film
56	The Prospector at the Chocolate Nugget Candy Factory
58	Reno's Genie
60	The Brüka Theatre
62	Believe in Burning Man Art
64	The Eddy
66	Galena Creek Bridge
68	Orson Hyde's Curse
70	Steamboat Hot Springs
72	Pyramid Lake Water Babies
74	Judas Priest: Subliminal Message Trial
76	Lincoln Highway Bridge Rails
78	Pyramid Lake: Two Legends and a Fish
80	That Terrible Thanksgiving
82	Lynched for a Murder That Didn't Happen
84	Harolds Club Wagon Trail Mural
104	Oxbow Nature Study Area
106	The Depot
108	Play Ball . . . Bocce Ball
110	The Silver Dollar Scandal
112	Shamrocks for Bill Blanchfield
114	Street Vibrations Motorcycle Spring and Fall Rally
116	Zebras, Tigers, and Shrunken Heads . . . Oh My!
118	Lucky Lindy Lands in Reno on September 19, 1927
120	Take Him Home Tonight

122	Ducks in a Row
124	Silver Baron's Silver Tea Set
126	At the Quad
128	James D. Hoff Peace Officer Memorial
130	Let the Games Begin
132	Atlas Isn't Shrugging
134	Shine On, Reno Star
136	Midtown District: A Bohemian Vibe
138	The Count and the Countess
140	The Galveston Giant Trounces the Great White Hope
142	Skyjacker
144	Sparks Marina Park
146	Scheels Ferris Wheel, Aquarium, and Arcade
148	Bat Bridge (McCarran Bridge)
150	The Volkswagen Bug
152	Last Chance Joe
154	Camel and Ostrich Races
156	Picon Punch and Poltergeists
158	World Championship Outhouse Races
160	Bigfoot
162	Mary Jane Simpson
164	Lady Justice Unblindfolded
166	Verdi: The Great Train Robbery
168	Mark Twain's Niece
170	Trick or Treat at the Governor's Mansion
172	Adam Uber's Curse
174	Spirit Cave Man

176	Tortoise and the Bottle Cap Gazebo
178	Black Rock City
180	Thunder Mountain Monument
182	Virginia City Mall
184	At the Drive-In
186	Never Enough Books
189	Sources
197	Index

ACKNOWLEDGMENTS

Special thanks to Debbie Bender, Kristin Hamlet, Dawn Grant, Dennis McBride, Rebecca Genesis, Cindy Hunt, Deny Dotson of the Virginia City Tourism Commission, Katie Demuth of the Virginia City Tourism Commission, Liza McIlwee, Virginia City Visitor Center, Mary Bennett, and last but certainly not least, my husband and photographer Bill Oberding.

INTRODUCTION

Welcome to Reno, the "Biggest Little City in the World," a rich and diverse city that offers something for just about everyone. You might say, and you'd be right, that Reno is a college town. The University of Nevada, Reno is located here, but there is so much more to see and do in the Biggest Little City. Bet you didn't know that Reno has a connection to Mount Rushmore or that you can go sailing in the middle of the Nevada desert. Although Samuel Clemens may have been born in Hannibal, it was Reno where he shed the family name and took on the nom de plume of Mark Twain. And what did Abraham Lincoln have to do with Mark Twain's literary career?

    Although more weddings than divorces took place here, Reno was once known as the divorce capital of the world. Where did recent divorcees dispose of their wedding rings? Hint, it wasn't the nearby pawn shop. In 1960, Marilyn Monroe, Clark Gable, Thelma Ritter, Eli Wallach, Montgomery Clift, and a large film crew came to town to film *The Misfits*. Written by Marilyn's husband playwright Arthur Miller, the black-and-white film wasn't a big hit with moviegoers. But why is this film said to be cursed?

    Is there a city in the middle of the Black Rock Desert that springs up like a desert oasis only to vanish after a week? Do you have to travel the 4,898 miles to Blarney Castle in Blarney, Ireland, just to kiss the Blarney Stone? Are you looking for a couple of haunted saloons that serve up Picon Punch with a bit of ghostly activity? Are you into the thrill of racing? What about World Championship Outhouse Races? You'll soon discover the answers to these questions and many more of Reno's secrets. So, grab your sunscreen and your water—Reno gets more than 300 days of sunshine each year, and hydration is important here in the high desert—and let's go explore this city.

A LITTLE RIVALRY

What's the heaviest and most expensive trophy in college football?

No doubt, explorer John C. Frémont would be very proud—or very surprised—that a replica of the howitzer cannon that accompanied him on his early 19th century expedition of the Western United States is today a sought after and fought over trophy. Built at a cost of $10,000, the cannon weighs in at a whopping 545 pounds, making it the most expensive and the heaviest trophy in college football.

The Frémont Cannon is the prize in the Battle for Nevada, an annual game between bitter rivals University of Nevada, Las Vegas (UNLV) and University of Nevada, Reno (UNR). It's all in good fun. The winning team takes possession of the cannon for the year, and the winner has the privilege of painting the cannon's carriage—either blue for UNR (the Wolf Pack) or red for UNLV (the Rebels).

Two famous alumni of UNR are Ron Toomer and Colin Kaepernick. Football star and activist Kaepernick is soon to be inducted into the University's Athletics Hall of Fame. Kaepernick played for the Wolf Pack for four years and achieved an outstanding record. If you've ever enjoyed a looping roller-coaster ride, you can thank Ron Toomer. Among those coasters beloved by daredevils, Toomer built the Corkscrew at Knott's Berry Farm, the Magnum XL-200 at Cedar Point, and the Big Bad Wolf of Busch Gardens.

Manzanita Lake at UNR

THAT'S A BIG TROPHY

WHAT: The Frémont Cannon

WHERE: Either at University of Nevada campus or University of Las Vegas campus (depending on who wins the Battle for Nevada football game)

COST: Free to see the cannon. Football games at UNR and UNLV will cost you.

PRO TIP: While visiting the University of Reno campus, be sure to stop and see Manzanita Lake with its swans, ducks, and turtles. The lake is near the Clark Administration Building.

Imagine how dejected the losing team feels when the victors take possession and wheel the cannon off the field. But not to worry, there's always next year!

If you're wondering what happened to the John C. Frémont expedition's original howitzer, it was abandoned high in the Sierra during a raging snowstorm in 1844. There it was left, buried deep beneath snow. Today, it can be seen in the Nevada State Museum in Carson City. How it got from atop the Sierra to Carson City is another story.

GENERAL JESSE L. RENO STATUE

Who is this Civil War general, and why is there a statue dedicated to him in downtown Reno?

Reno is his namesake, never mind that General Jesse Lee Reno never set foot in the city. The good general never even visited Nevada. Maybe he would have, but he never got the chance. The heroic Union general was killed during the Antietam campaign in the fight for Fox's Gap on September 14, 1862, six years before the city named after him was founded on May 9, 1868.

Thus, he would never visit the city that bears his name here in Nevada. However, General Reno maintained his sense of humor until the end. As the mortally wounded Reno was being carried on a stretcher past his friend Brigadier General Samuel D. Sturgis, he cried out, "Hallo, Sam, I'm dead!"

When Sturgis said, "It's not that bad."

Reno replied, "Yes, yes, I'm dead, goodbye!"

Unfortunately, General Reno was correct. But the Biggest Little City remembers, and General Jesse L. Reno hasn't been forgotten. On Memorial Day in 2006, a statue of General Reno was unveiled at Powning Park in downtown Reno. As far as parks go, Powning Veteran's Memorial Park is a very small park near the

HOMAGE TO A UNION GENERAL

WHAT: The General Jesse L. Reno Statue

WHERE: Powning Veteran Memorial Park (downtown Reno), 150 S Virginia St.

COST: Free

PRO TIP: While at the tiny Powning Park, look across the intersection of S Virginia and Mill Streets at the Pioneer Center for the Performing Arts. Locals call this unusual building the Golden Turtle.

Pioneer Center for the Performing Arts (the Golden Turtle), Historic Post Office, and City Hall are in the background.

Pioneer Center for the Performing Arts and catty-corner to the Washoe County Courthouse. As far as cities go, General Jesse Lee Reno would no doubt be very proud of his namesake.

The Pioneer Center for the Performing Arts is the site of the former Nevada State Building. On October 12, 1964, while running for reelection after the JFK assassination, Lyndon Baines Johnson came to town and gave a campaign speech on the steps of the old state building. Two years later, the building was razed. The only thing left was the 1939 statue of the pioneer family, which was moved nearer to Virginia St.—that's why it was named the Pioneer Center for the Performing Arts.

KISS THE COURTHOUSE PILLAR

Why did she kiss the courthouse pillar?

Over time her name's been lost to history, but, whoever she was, the first woman to kiss one of the pillars outside the Washoe County Courthouse was probably superstitious and thinking of that old proverb "lucky in cards, unlucky in love." Maybe she was so thrilled to be out of an unhappy marriage that she stopped and gave the pillar a big smooch. Or maybe she hoped that kiss would bring her good luck when she chose her next mate. Whatever she may have been thinking, this newly minted divorcee started a Reno custom. Kissing the Pillar was soon so popular with divorcees that *Life* magazine featured a model kissing a pillar on the cover of its June 21, 1937, issue. Some might argue that it was actually the *Life* magazine cover that gave rise to the Reno tradition, and perhaps it was. Yet, kissing a courthouse pillar was soon the fashionable thing for a divorcee to do.

   That was a lot of kisses. Thanks to Nevada's easy divorce laws and quickie divorces, divorce was big business in the early 20th century here in Reno, the former Divorce Capital of the World. Once her six week's residency was behind her and the divorce was official, a woman probably hoped for better luck in a matrimonial endeavor next time around.

> At one time, the Washoe County Jail was located on a top floor of the courthouse. In 1974, bank robber Floyd Clayton Forsberg and another man made a daring escape from this jail by climbing out of a vent and placing a ladder across the roof of the jail to that of the Riverside Hotel.

Kissable pillars at the Washoe County Courthouse

I DO–I DON'T

WHAT: The Washoe County Courthouse

WHERE: 117 S Virginia St.

COST: Free

PRO TIP: Enter the courthouse through the side door on Court St. Take the stairway to the second floor and a view of what lies beneath the copper dome—a beautiful intricate stained glass design. FYI: "Washoe" rhymes with "light snow."

Being wise enough to realize that kind of luck wasn't found in the gambling halls that lined N Virginia St., she stepped up to the pillar and gave it a go.

Did the custom bring good luck? Maybe it did, and maybe it didn't. According to one Reno rumor, blonde actress Marilyn Monroe kissed a courthouse pillar when she was in town filming *The Misfits* in 1961. Because there are no photographs of the event, that story must remain in the rumor file.

WEDDING RING BRIDGE LEGEND

Is that gold sparkling in the water?

Every city has its legends, and Reno is no exception. Because of Nevada's short residency requirements divorce was a booming business from the early to the mid-20th century in Reno. Divorce also proved to be a lucrative business for lawyers, shopkeepers, and landlords alike. The Wedding Ring Bridge legend is yet another legend that involves divorce.

It may have been started by someone suffering from gold fever and looking for an easy way to pan for the precious metal. In theory it sounded perfectly logical. Nevada is, after all, a state known for its early days of silver and gold rushes. And so, the story went that once she was officially divorced, a woman was supposed to walk the few yards from the Washoe County Courthouse to the bridge that spans the Truckee River. There she was to divest herself of the offending wedding ring. Many divorcees were superstitious enough to do just that. Never mind that there were plenty of pawn shops ready, willing, and able to buy the little bands of gold. The romance was over, and the ring was only a reminder of what might have been. What good was the

GOLD IS WHERE YOU FIND IT

WHAT: The Virginia Street Bridge

WHERE: Walk north a block from the Washoe County Courthouse. The exact spot is lost to history. Best guess it was on the west side of the old Virginia Street Bridge just across the street from the Riverside Artists Loft.

COST: Free

PRO TIP: There is a scene in the 1960 film *The Misfits* in which Marilyn Monroe as Roslyn and Thelma Ritter as Isabelle are on the bridge and discussing tossing a ring into the river.

The new Reno Bridge

ring now? So, newly divorced women stood on the bridge, made that leap of faith and tossed their rings into the Truckee River. They may have gone back home or stayed in Reno and put down roots. One thing they all did was to move on with their lives.

But not to worry, those little bands of gold didn't stay put in the depths of the river for long. It's only fair to tell you that there were those (usually teenage boys) who made a bit of side money by combing the river for gold rings, but no one does that anymore . . . they say.

The bridge is also referred to as the bridge of sighs. In the 1939 film *Reno* starring Richard Dix, Gail Patrick, and Anita Louise, one of the characters gets her divorce, walks to the bridge, and tosses her ring into the Truckee River.

THE BIGGEST LITTLE CITY IN THE WORLD

What's in a name?

So, we all know that Reno is the Biggest Little City in the World. But have you ever wondered just how it got that name? In the early 1900s, Renoites, eager to draw tourists, started calling their city the "biggest little city on the map." Geography aside, that slogan doesn't have much allure. It doesn't exactly make anyone want to jump in a car, board a train or a plane, and visit Reno. Some savvy Renoites replaced the word "map" with "world."

But the Reno City Council and Mayor E. E. Roberts wanted something more formal. So, in 1929, the council announced a contest for a slogan, but they received no entries until money was offered as an incentive. The prize would be $100, which was big money in 1929. In poured the entries, and in March, G. A. Burns of Sacramento, California, was declared the contest winner with his slogan, "Reno, the Biggest Little City in the World." That sounded right and apropos for a city with fewer than 20,000 residents. On June 25, 1929, it was official; the words "The Biggest Little City in

---

> E. E. (Edwin Ewing) Roberts was one of Reno's most colorful mayors. He served from 1923 to 1933. He was a divorce attorney who saw divorce as necessary, and he intensely disliked gambling and Prohibition. When he debated a proponent of Prohibition at a local church on March 29, 1931, Roberts said, "If I had my way, I'd place a barrel of whiskey on every corner with a dipper and a sign saying, 'Help yourself, but don't be a hog.'"

Old Reno Arch

the World" appeared in lights on the Reno Arch for the first time. Movies filmed here began to incorporate the arch and those words into a scene or two, thereby associating the arch and its slogan with Reno.

The population of Reno has increased more than tenfold since G. A. Burns accepted his prize money, and the slogan is as fitting today as it was then. The Biggest Little City in the World is one moniker that has survived the test of time.

AN OLDIE BUT A GOODIE

WHAT: The Old Reno Arch

WHERE: On Lake St. (at the Truckee River)

COST: Free

PRO TIP: Any time is a great time to visit Reno. Festivals rule year round. In the summer there is Artown, Hot August Nights (old cars rock n' roll and 1950s nostalgia), Biggest Little City Wing Fest, and more. The fall is The National Championship Air Races and the Balloon Races. Winter offers great skiing in the Lake Tahoe area, a mere hour away.

THE BLARNEY STONE...
A PIECE OF IT ANYWAY

Will it bring good luck?

According to an old Irish legend, anyone who wants the gift of gab and charm will have to kiss the Blarney Stone. Millions of people have trusted in the legend, gone to the castle, and kissed the stone since Francis Grose first wrote about the legend in the 1785 work, *A Classical Dictionary of the Vulgar Tongue*. The Blarney Stone is located at Blarney Castle in Blarney, Ireland—only about 4,898 miles from Reno.

If Ireland's a bit far, there is another way. You can go to the Whitney Peak Hotel in downtown Reno (near the arch). There a piece of the original Blarney Stone has been embedded in a front wall of the hotel since the 1980s when Fitzgerald's owned the building. This is the real deal. It's not a gimmick. If you doubt the stone's authenticity, note that a dedication was made on St. Patrick's Day (March 17th) in 1988 by the Northern Nevada Chapter of the Sons of Erin—and that makes it official.

> ### SURE AND BEGORRAH
>
> **WHAT:** A bit of the Blarney Stone
> **WHERE:** Whitney Peak Hotel, 255 N Virginia St.
> **COST:** Free
> **PRO TIP:** The stone is placed a tad high on the wall for those vertically challenged. Be on your tiptoes or wear heels if this applies to you.

Whitney Peak is unique in downtown Reno in that it's both a nonsmoking and nongaming hotel.

Blarney Stone

Reno is a gambling city, and its traditions have nothing to do with gab and charm. Besides, you don't need those qualities to win big in the casinos. However, if you should want good luck in your gaming endeavors, touch the stone and make a wish. Perhaps you'll win a bundle. Then again, maybe you won't. Still, you won't have to book a flight and travel 4,898 miles to kiss the Blarney Stone.

WORLD'S TALLEST ARTIFICIAL CLIMBING WALL

What if I don't know anything about climbing?

Look up—all the way up. Why are all those people climbing up the side of the building? They are getting in shape at BaseCamp at the Whitney Peak Hotel. Regardless your skill level, BaseCamp offers an array of fitness and climbing classes from beginner to advanced climbers. Skip the gym today and try a different exercise routine. There are so many reasons to visit Reno, especially if you're an outdoor enthusiast. Those who come looking for a unique challenge are sure to find it at the 164-foot climbing wall on the side of Whitney Peak Hotel. And just so you know, for the record, it happens to officially be the tallest artificial climbing wall in the world according to the *Guinness Book of World Records*. Can

---

Lincoln Fitzgerald opened his Fitzgerald's Reno in 1976. Fitzgerald died in 1981, and the hotel was eventually sold. In 2014, it was remodeled and opened as Whitney Peak Hotel. Lincoln Fitzgerald was a colorful early-day Nevada gaming figure. He was said to have been a member of Detroit's infamous Purple Gang, who ran a successful illegal gaming operation in Michigan. With legalized gambling going strong in Nevada, Fitzgerald and his partner moved here in 1945 to avoid prosecution in Michigan.

Climbing Wall

SOCIAL CLIMBERS DELIGHT

WHAT: BaseCamp

WHERE: Whitney Peak Hotel, 255 N Virginia St.

COST: Fees vary

PRO TIP: Climbing is best done on a clear calm day.

you imagine telling friends back home that you came to Reno and of the many fun things you did, you climbed the tallest climbing wall in the world? There is nothing wrong with boasting if you are brave enough to tackle the tallest artificial climbing wall in the world. When you're ready, the wall is waiting for the adventuresome to come and climb.

LAZY DAYS ON THE TRUCKEE

Can I kayak in the city?

A river runs through it, and the city of Reno takes full advantage of the Truckee River. The Truckee starts its descent high in the Sierra, flowing down into Reno and out to Pyramid Lake where it's swallowed in the vast saltwater lake.

Wingfield Park is a great place to enjoy the river whether you wade into it or lounge on the grass and gaze at sunlight sparkling on the water. Bring the family and a picnic to make a day of it. There is a sectioned off part of the river for the kiddies that isn't too deep or fast moving.

The more adventuresome should know that the temperature of the Truckee ranges from 50 to 70 degrees,

ROLLING ALONG ON THE RIVER

WHAT: Wingfield Park

WHERE: 2 S Arlington St. (downtown)

COST: Equipment rental costs vary, generally starting at $25 per day.

PRO TIP: FYI, "Truckee" rhymes with "lucky."

In an 1842 exploration of the Great Basin, John C. Frémont named the Truckee the Salmon Trout River for the large trout that inhabited the river. The name didn't stick. Eventually, the river was named Truckee in honor of a Paiute chief who guided a group of emigrants along the river to Donner Lake in 1844.

Truckee River

which is close to perfect for watersports. Kayaking is king here. But those who want to canoe, raft, or just float along on an inner tube can also enjoy the river as it makes its way through downtown Reno. Reno's Truckee River Whitewater Park at Wingfield offers a course that is a half-mile long and is rated a 2-3 level of difficulty.

Kayaking, like all sports, has its own jargon. Maneuvers enjoyed by kayakers include freestyle cartwheeling, splatting, and front flips. There is a difference between canoes and kayaks. Don't despair if you don't know the difference or one end of a kayak from the other, as licensed instructors and rentals are available in the city and at the park.

JEANS

What goes with jeans?

According to an old saying necessity is the mother of invention. This is definitely true in the case of jeans. If not for a housewife trying to save herself some time and money, none of us would be wearing jeans. Can you imagine a world without jeans? I can't.

Jeans are part of our culture. Every fashionista knows that they are acceptable in any circumstance. The martini and the fortune cookie may have been invented in San Francisco, but jeans were not. Jeans were invented right here in downtown Reno, Nevada. A Reno tailor by the name of Jacob Davis (Jacob Youphes) is responsible for creating jeans. If you'd like to see the exact spot where Jacob Davis created his iconic idea, there is a plaque honoring him and his work at the location on a N Virginia St. sidewalk.

The story goes that in 1870 the wife of a woodcutter came to Jacob Davis's shop with a request. Would it be possible to make a pair of trousers with seams sturdy enough to withstand her burly husband whose work kept tearing his seams open? Not one to shy away from a challenge, Davis assured the beleaguered housewife that of course he could . . . and he did.

Using heavy duck fabric he'd purchased from the Levi Strauss & Co., Davis worked into the night creating the pants. He was almost finished when he came up with an idea that would forever change the fashion industry. For good measure, Davis ingeniously reinforced the seams with copper rivets. If this wouldn't hold the

---

In 1867, Jacob Davis was operating a cigar store in Virginia City. He decided to move to Reno in 1868 and return to his work as a tailor.

Jeans Plaque

seams nothing would. Word soon got out and Jacob Davis faced a heavy workload. Soon everyone wanted a pair of sturdy trousers. Davis kept busy making the reinforced jeans until his work came to the attention of Levi Strauss who offered him a lucrative partnership deal. And the rest is fashion history.

There are so many different styles and colors of jeans. Skinny, boot top, and straight leg, none are anything like the original jeans. If you're curious to see what the originals looked like, you should know that the Levi Strauss Company still has a few pairs of Jacob Davis original copper-riveted jeans. They take them on tour from time to time.

SEW WHAT

WHAT: The Jeans Plaque
WHERE: 211 N Virginia St.
COST: Free
PRO TIP: Across the street from the plaque, is the all-new Reno City Center, which is slated for completion in 2022. The Reno City Center will feature office space, a gym, shops, a bar, a coffee shop, a grocery store, and apartments. Wonder what Mr. Davis would have made of that.

THE DONNER PARTY CAMPED HERE

Why was the Donner Party fascinated with Reno?

Most everyone in this area knows the story of the unfortunate Donner Party. En route to California with its vast farmland, the Donner Party got stranded in a deadly snow blizzard atop the Sierra Nevada. When they ran out of livestock and food supplies, they survived by cannibalizing dead members of the party. No one likes to think of ordinary people becoming cannibals, but it happened. Science and history have proven this. All's well that ends well, and those who lived through the ordeal saw their California dreams come to fruition. None of it might have happened if only they hadn't stayed in what is present day Reno so long.

After the long and harrowing journey, they arrived in late summer of 1843. Water was plentiful, and the weather was mild. Camping at the base of what is known today as Rattlesnake Mountain, they lulled themselves into believing the worst was behind them, so they postponed the last leg of their journey—that was a fateful mistake. There is a plaque honoring the Donners at the Millcreek Townhomes neighborhood in Southeast Reno. As you stop to ponder the fate that awaited the Donner Party high up in the Sierra, listen close and you may hear just the wind . . . or the

LAST RESPITE

WHAT: The Donner Party Memorial

WHERE: Donner Party Park Rio Pico Rd. and Loreto Ln., Mill Creek Townhomes Village

COST: Free

PRO TIP: This is a small park wedged into a residential location. Parking is at a premium. Being careful not to go onto private property, you can walk to the spot between townhomes at the base of Rattlesnake Mountain where the Donners made camp.

Rattlesnake Mountain where Donner Party camped

ghostly cries of a member of the Donner Party. Some who live in this neighborhood occasionally see what appears to be a ghost near the trees at the campsite.

It would be remiss not to mention that anyone who is truly interested in the Donner Party should visit the Donner State Park 35 miles west of Reno (and in California). There is an all-new museum, walking trail, monument, and large memorial where the family camped and cannibalized the dead.

WINDY HILL (AUDREY HARRIS PARK)

Where's a romantic spot to pop the question?

Sometimes, it's necessary to get a different perspective. In Reno there is no better place to do so than Windy Hill at Audrey Harris Park. Those who've lived in Reno any length of time know this is a spot that offers one of the best views in Reno day or night. Renoites in the know have been driving up here with their sweeties for decades to park, talk romance, and take in the view of the city's lights far below, especially at night. Many a Reno area lover has probably popped the question while parked here at Windy Hill. Yes, this is one of those places where marriage proposals are accepted — or rejected.

The parking area has been revamped and expanded over the years. There are approximately 15 parking spaces and park benches, so you will seldom encounter a crowd. Well, except after dark on the Fourth of July. Fireworks

> ### LOVER'S SPOT
>
> **WHAT:** Windy Hill
>
> **WHERE:** 6600 Lakeside Dr.
>
> **COST:** Free
>
> **PRO TIP:** The historic Huffaker School is located at Bartley Ranch Regional Park, which features multiuse trails, horse arenas, barbecuing, and picnicking. The trail is easy going down, but don't forget that you'll be walking up on your return trip.

Windy Hill figured prominently in a horrific Reno murder when killer Thomas Lee Bean drove up to the hill to dispose of evidence in the 1963 murder of Sonja McCaskie.

View from Windy Hill, Audrey Harris Park

are not a given in Reno with high winds and the fire danger. But if there happens to be fireworks, there will be so many cars trying to squeeze in for a bird's-eye view of the firework displays that it's hardly worth the effort.

This is a small park in a somewhat rural area. You may occasionally encounter horseback riders during the day. If you're coming up to Windy Hill during daylight hours for a getaway brown bag lunch and some fresh air, you can get some exercise by taking the half hour walk down to Bartley Ranch Regional Park. It's not a very long walk.

THE GAZEBO AT HUFFAKER MOUNTAIN

Where can you get some exercise in the city while in the midst of rugged nature?

Look around; here you are and city sprawl is all around. And yet you're in a spot that hasn't been touched by progress, except for the trail designations, the signs, and the gazebo. At Huffaker Mountain Trail, you're in the city, yet you're surrounded by desert flora and fauna. Put your comfy shoes on and bring a bottle of water because you're going to do some walking for this one. If you're going to bring your dog, and there's no reason why you shouldn't, please be aware that Fido must be on a leash. It's the law. And besides that, you don't want your dog chasing and harassing wildlife. You're going to do some walking to get to the gazebo. But it will be worth it. The trail is rocky and there's no shade, making this walk best done in the early morning hours or late in the afternoon. On most days you will encounter other hikers and their dogs. Most are courteous and have their dogs on leashes, but be aware not all do. This is Nevada, so sagebrush is everywhere. But in spring, there are also

READY FOR A WALK

WHAT: Huffaker Mountain Trail
WHERE: 7550 Offenhauser Dr.
COST: Free
PRO TIP: Bring a lunch and have a picnic at the tables placed at different locations on the trail.

> Huffaker Mountain Trail picks up at Huffaker Park with a small play area for the kids, shaded areas, basketball hoops, and an expanse of grass.

Huffaker Mountain Trail

wildflowers and a few scraggly cactus plants along the way. Stay on the trail, and be on the lookout for squirrels, jackrabbits, and lizards as you walk. Occasionally a snake may slither across the walking trail. These seem to be of the harmless garden variety, but since only a herpetologist knows for sure, be mindful and step lightly.

Look at all the steps you've achieved. When you've made it to the top, take a rest and look around at the gazebo. The views are incredible in all directions; overhead, you might catch sight of a red tail hawk in search of a slow moving rodent or rabbit. To the west are Mt. Rose and Slide Mountain. Plane watchers are in for a treat. To the north, you can clearly see the runways of the Reno Tahoe International Airport and, on any given day, see and hear airplanes taking off and landing.

To the northwest is Peavine Mountain. Is it covered with snow or not? Every Reno gardener knows the old saying that you "don't plant tomatoes until the snow is off Peavine." If you should heedlessly plant anyway, don't say you weren't warned when the frost kills your tender seedlings.

WA-PAI-SHONE AT ROSE GARDEN IDLEWILD PARK

Where can you take a selfie with Wa-Pai-Shone, Reno's whispering giant?

The quest for a great selfie is second nature to most of us. I'm not sure what that says about our society. But if you have a selfie stick and a little ingenuity, you can take a great selfie with Reno's whispering giant located at Idlewild Park between the Rose Garden and the Peace Officer Memorial.

Everyone can pose with their cat or dog. And those make for sweet shots, but you've got to admit that not everyone can take a selfie with something as unusual as Wa-Pai-Shone. Wa-Pai-Shone is a 17-foot wood carving depicting a Native American man who seems to be happy and at peace with his surroundings. The name Wa-Pai-Shone is a compilation of the three tribes of Nevada: the Washoe, the Paiute, and the Shoshone.

Each of these three tribes played an integral part in Nevada's history. As a way to honor all the indigenous people who lived on this land long before the rest of us, Hungarian-born, artist Peter Wolf Toth traveled across North America creating his collection,

---

Adjacent to Wa-Pai-Shone is the Rose Garden with more than 200 varieties of roses. It's the only rose garden in the state of Nevada to be certified by the American Rose Society.

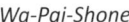

Wa-Pai-Shone

LOTS TO SEE

WHAT: Idlewild Park

WHERE: 1900 Idlewild Dr.

COST: Free

PRO TIP: If you're looking for shade in the heat of summer, this is one of Reno's few parks with large shade trees and an expanse of grass. You'll also find the Rose Garden and the Kiddie Park at Idlewild Park.

known as Trail of Whispering Giants, which consisted of 74 chain saw carved wood sculptures (Whispering Giants).

Toth completed his Douglas fir carving of Wa-Pai-Shone, the 53rd in the series in June 1986. Since that time countless people have come to see Wa-Pai-Shone and to pose for a photo with the whispering giant which some say has the happiest face of all the whispering giants. Wa-Pai-Shone also is listed in the Smithsonian Art Inventory Catalog.

NATIONAL BOWLING STADIUM, INTERNATIONAL BOWLING MUSEUM & HALL OF FAME (RENO SATELLITE)

How can I find the National Bowling Stadium?

Although people have been bowling, playing a similar game, for centuries, none of them could have imagined the National Bowling Stadium in Reno. It's one of the easiest landmarks in Reno to find. Just look for the big aluminum geodesic dome on top of the building, representing a bowling ball, the unique 80-foot dome gives a very different perspective to the Reno skyline.

Reno is proud of its National Bowling Stadium which happens to be one of a kind. Not in Paris, Rome, or Las Vegas, is there another facility like it in the world.

ONE OF ONE

WHAT: National Bowling Stadium

WHERE: 300 N Center St.

COST: Free

PRO TIP: The stadium lanes are only for tournament players' use, but the museum is open to the public.

If there's a bowling scene in a film, odds are it was filmed at the National Bowling Stadium. The stadium's nickname is the "Taj Mahal of Tenpins," but at a cost of $47.5 million that's about 47 times more than its eponym the Taj Mahal cost to build back in 1632.

Bowling Stadium

Built in 1995 for tournament bowling, the 363,000 square foot stadium offers 78 lanes, and can be used for other events as well.

Bowlers from all over the world come to Reno to bowl at the unique stadium. Tournament players know that the International Bowling Museum & Hall of Fame (Reno Satellite) is located in the stadium as well. The museum is the only such branch of the International Bowling Museum & Hall of Fame. Learn some bowling history and see photos of championship bowlers from back in the day.

THE LEAR THEATER

Does Reno have diversity in architecture?

In 1957, distinguished African American architect Paul Revere Williams became the first African American to be voted a fellow of the American Institute of Architects. In 1939, years before that honor was bestowed upon him, Williams was commissioned to design the First Church of Christ, Scientist on Riverside Dr. across from the Truckee River on the edge of downtown Reno. The resulting building was Neoclassical in style and would serve the congregation for the next 59 years.

In 1998 Moya Lear, widow of famed pioneering aviation inventor Bill Lear Jr., had an idea. She would pledge a million dollars toward the purchase of the church building if the community would match her million. It did and the building was turned over to the Reno Sparks theater community. The plan was for the building to be renovated and repurposed for use as a theater. Because of Moya Lear's generosity, the theater would be named the Lear Theater. In 2011, after several million dollars was spent, the building was given to Artown. For the next few years, performances took place in the Lear Theater.

Fast forward to the present and the Lear Theater is in trouble. Vandals have wreaked havoc with the building; it is old and in bad need of costly repairs. The Lear Theater sits on a prime

---

> Among Williams's designs are the iconic Los Angeles International Airport theme building and the La Concha Motel lobby in Las Vegas (restored at the Neon Museum in Las Vegas). Another Reno example of his work is the Loomis Manor Apartments on 1045 Riverside Dr.

Lear Theater

piece of downtown real estate. Developers anticipate the day when Artown may cut its losses and sell the property, in which case it will be razed to make room for an apartment building.

Preservationists are hoping this won't ever come to pass. The Lear Theater is significant both historically and culturally. It is a fine example of Paul Revere Williams's work. Although there are thousands of examples of his work in the Los Angeles area, only a few other buildings and residences of Williams's design are still standing in Reno today.

DIVERSITY IN ART

WHAT: Lear Theater

WHERE: 538 W First St.

COST: Free

PRO TIP: Not a lot of parking is available here. It's best to park on Riverside Dr. (if you can find a place) or Arlington St. and do some walking.

ARTOWN

What does the artsy crowd do in July?

July is Reno's hottest month. But it isn't just a month of one lazy sweltering day after another. July is the month that local art lovers look forward to every year. From the first day of July until the last, artists from around the block and around the world showcase their talents through dance, music, film, theater, and workshops during Artown here in the Biggest Little City. From concerts, plays, films, dancing, and an art show or two, there's bound to be something on the Artown agenda that you and the entire family will enjoy.

Artown is funded by the Nevada Arts Council and the National Endowment for the Arts. It began as a way to revitalize downtown Reno in 1996. From its onset, the festival has been a success, bringing thousands of people to different venues throughout the city. Artown focuses both on adults and children. One family favorite is music in the park. Bring a picnic lunch and listen to some good music. Ballet that rocks, ukulele, drums and old movies, mix with dancers like Bandaloop (pioneer vertical dancers), and musicians like the Mexican/American rock band Los Lobos, have all been part of Artown.

The festival takes place downtown in Wingfield Park and at various other locations throughout the city.

> **TAKE YOUR PICK**
>
> **WHAT:** Artown
>
> **WHERE:** Wingfield Park Downtown Reno and various other locations
>
> **COST:** Both free and paid entertainment
>
> **PRO TIP:** Get there early. If you're interested in a free event that starts at 7 p.m., for example, get there, stake out your spot, or line up by 5 p.m. Yes, it's that popular.

Crowd enjoying an early evening concert at the amphiteater at Wingfield Park during Artown.

Some of the artists that have appeared at Artown since it began in 1996 are Marcel Marceau, Harlem Gospel Choir, Dat Phan, and Mikhail Baryshnikov.

VIRGINIA LAKE

Where can you enjoy nature in the midst of the busy city?

So, you're on Lakeside Dr. at Virginia Lake, traffic is stopped, and you're in a hurry. What's the hold up? There's not a pedestrian in sight, and the car in front of you isn't stalled or otherwise broken down. Before you can honk your disapproval, traffic is moving once again. You absently glance to your left and see it: a mother duck followed by six little ducklings was crossing the street. Ducks rule here at Virginia Lake that was created in 1937 with help from the Civilian Conservation Corps as part of the New Deal. The lake was built specifically for fishing, and it's stocked with trout, rainbow and brown, every season.

But times have changed. Today, there are lots of other things to do here besides fish and watch ducks. There are picnic tables, a few scattered pieces of Burning Man art, and a kiddie playground. Those who like to stay active will like the jogging and walking trail that encircles the lake. There are other exercise areas, a doggie park, and barbeque pits. The lake is not large. It covers approximately 24 acres. At its deepest, it is only 12 feet deep.

REEL 'EM IN

WHAT: Virginia Lake

WHERE: 1980 Lakeside Dr. (just west of the Peppermill Hotel)

COST: Free to visit. But if you're fishing, a license is $80 annually for nonresidents or $18 a day (cost is half these prices for locals).

PRO TIP: If you've got little ones with you, there is a small playground across Lakeside Dr..

Virginia Lake

Getting back to its original purpose, fishing, they say, is good here at Virginia Lake—especially if you bait your hook with night crawlers. But don't forget that you'll need a license to fish here, or anywhere in Reno for that matter.

When Virginia Lake was created, it was considered to be on the edge of town. The city has grown up around the lake with the Peppermill Hotel Casino around the corner and Reno's all-new Reno Experience District (RED) luxury apartments, a park, a hotel, and shopping.

GIANT POKER CHIPS

Where can you sit?

You won't be here long before you realize that there is much to see and do in downtown Reno. At some point while you're exploring, your feet may beg for a rest. This is when you may want to just sit and take it all in. If you happen to be at the corner of Virginia St. and Commercial Row near the arch, you're in luck, in a city where luck is everything. Aching feet, there's a piece of artwork for that. There's a piece of artwork that is a great spot just waiting for you: a stack of giant poker chips made of concrete and glaze porcelain mosaic.

Unlike the Mona Lisa these chips are artwork that can be enjoyed while also serving a strictly utilitarian purpose. Every photographer who has ever visited Reno has stopped somewhere near the Reno Arch, hoping for that one great shot while resting their feet. Slot machines and 24/7 bars are everywhere in the Biggest Little City. Balancing this out is the ubiquitous works of art throughout the city. The giant poker chips is but one of the over 185 works of art, both temporary and permanent that the city showcases throughout the city, proving that Reno may be a college town and a gambling city, but clearly it's also a city that embraces art.

The giant poker chips sculpture is the creation of local artist Eileen Gay. The sculpture is called In the Chips; Fate, Luck and Magic. And I can't think of a more apropos name considering Reno gained notoriety for its glitz, gambling, and quickie divorces,

---

HAVE A SEAT

WHAT: Giant Poker Chips Street Art

WHERE: Downtown at the corner of Virginia St. and Commercial Row

COST: Free

PRO TIP: If you want to take some photos of the Reno Arch, this is a great spot to do so.

Giant poker chips

long before Las Vegas put up its first neon sign. Back in the day, gamblers, divorcees, and newlyweds flocked to the Biggest Little City hoping for a little luck and a lot of magic. So tell me, who couldn't use a little luck and magic while also being on the good side of fate?

> Reno's Southern Pacific Railroad Depot built in 1926 is located at 135 E Commercial Row. Commercial Row is the location of many of Reno's early gambling halls.

MISS WAKAYAMA AND THE TWO-HEADED CALF

Where can I learn local history in a fun way?

The Nevada Historical Society in Reno is a wonderful place to spend an afternoon learning more about Reno and Nevada's history. The historical society has many unique historic items on display, including gambling devices from the early 20th century, Native American artifacts, and early day Reno items. Two displays draw a lot of attention, especially from school-age children. The first is the two-headed calf that suffered from the condition known as polycephaly, literally meaning having more than one head. It's a rarity for sure. The calf has been around a long time. The other favored display is the 3-foot-tall Miss Wakayama doll.

In 1927, the United States sent 12,739 American dolls to Japan. Two years later, Japan reciprocated with 58 Japanese dolls that were sent to libraries and museums across the United States. The Miss Wakayama doll is the friendship doll given to the

---

Fleischmann Planetarium and Science Center was funded by the Max C. Fleischmann Foundation. It was named after Charles Louis Fleischmann, creator of the first commercially produced yeast in the United States, whose son Max founded the foundation. The planetarium opened in 1964 and is listed in the National Register of Historic Places. It was the first planetarium in the United States to offer a 360-degree projector with stunning horizon-to-horizon views.

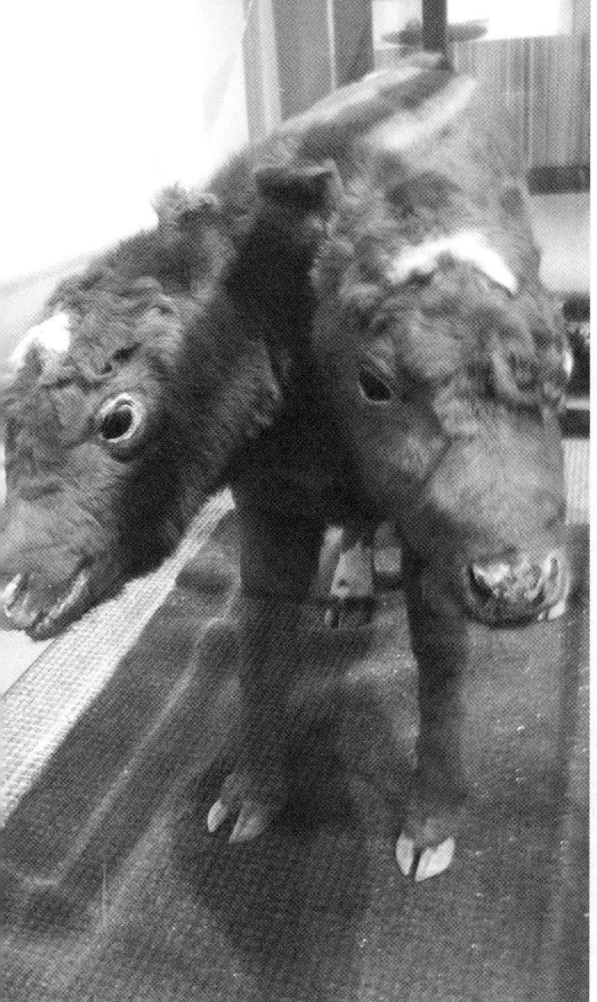

Two-headed calf

A PAST AND A PRESENT

WHAT: Nevada Historical Society

WHERE: On the UNR Campus, 1650 N Virginia St.

COST: $5 per adult; free to kids 17 and under

PRO TIP: Parking is at a premium and strictly enforced. To visit two great locations while using one parking space, it's good to know that the Fleischmann Planetarium and Science Center is within walking distance.

Nevada Historical Society from Japan in 1929. She is one of the 46 extant friendship dolls in the United States today. She has been on display ever since, except of course during World War II, when the United States and Japan were at war with each other.

Anyone wishing to do in-depth research of a specific topic of Reno or Nevada history will be happy in the research library at the Nevada Historical Society.

GIDDY UP

Wanna be a cowboy?

Does a cowpoke singing "Whoopie-ti-yi-yo, get along you little dogies" pull at your heartstrings? Then think about the Reno Cattle Drive. It is the ideal vacation for anyone who's ever dreamed of dressing up in boots, hat, and spurs and living the cowboy lifestyle. But fair warning, this isn't going to be like a vacation at some four-star hotel, complete with room service, plush bath robes, slippers, and spa. This is a working vacation—your chance to sleep under the stars, eat from the chuck wagon and to live just like the cowboys of the old west. And there will be no sleeping in, or dodging inclement weather. Rain, snow, or shine, the cattle drive starts out at the crack of dawn in Doyle, California, 45 miles north of Reno. It happens in mid-June, but that's no guarantee that the weather will be mild or warm. This is Northern Nevada and the weather can change dramatically from one day to the next.

Five days after it heads out, the 300 head of cattle and the 60 or so hardy participants arrive in Reno to cheering crowds along the sidewalks of Oddie Blvd., McCarran, and Sutro. Wyatt Earp never had it so good.

A COWPOKE'S DREAM

WHAT: The Reno Cattle Drive

WHERE: To see the cattle drive, locations include Oddie Blvd., Sutro, and McCarran.

COST: Free to watch (so get to your spot early); $2,000 per person to participate in the five-day cattle drive. Rules and required cowboy attire are specific.

For application and more info:
Reno Rodeo Cattle Drive
Reno Rodeo Association
P.O. Box 12335
Reno, NV 89510

PRO TIP: Hurry, space is very limited and fills up fast. Email renorodeocattledrive@gmail.com for more information

The Reno Cattle Drive. Photos by Cindy Hunt

Even if you can't see yourself spending eight hours a day in a saddle, and don't want to work at being a real cowboy, the cattle drive is a great photo op and chance to watch cattle, cowboys, and a few horse-or mule-drawn wagons make their way down city streets. The annual Reno Cattle Drive is one fun way to kick off the Reno Rodeo. Saddle up and head 'em out!

We can't saddle up without a mention of Nevada's cowboy Rex Bell. Bell was the star of numerous westerns in the 1920s and 1930s. He was married to silent film star Clara Bow the It girl, owned a western clothing store in Reno and a ranch in the Las Vegas area. He was also the 21st Lieutenant Governor of Nevada.

RENO RODEO

Who wants to watch some real out West action?

Through a geographical quirk, Reno is further west than Los Angeles. In spite of this, the city has always enjoyed its western status, especially during rodeo season, which is 10 days in June.

Established in 1919 as the Reno Round-Up, the Reno Rodeo is Reno's longest running special event and one of Renoites all-time favorites. With the rodeo comes the western spirit. Look for cowboys and cowgirls all over town. It's not difficult to spot locals wearing their best cowboy boots and hats, while some opt to wear full western attire. Many local businesses relax their standard uniform requirements, permitting employees to get into the spirit of the Reno Rodeo and dress western.

Billed as the Wildest Richest Rodeo in the West, the 10-day annual Reno Rodeo is a Professional Rodeo Cowboys Association (PRCA) sanctioned event. It's also a western lover's dream come true, not to mention all those tourist dollars being spent.

Ruling over the rodeo is the lovely Miss Reno Rodeo, a local young woman chosen for her appearance, poise, and horsemanship. You're fixing to have some fun when you grab your cowboy hat and come on out to

---

TEN GALLON HATS AND BUCKING BRONCS

WHAT: Reno Rodeo

WHERE: Reno Livestock Events Center, 1350 N Wells

COST: Tickets can run $100 and up depending on the day you choose to go and where you want to sit.

PRO TIP: If you're really serious about the rodeo, you can become a member of the Reno Rodeo Association. To be considered for membership you will need to fill out a wrangler application (to volunteer) and do so for two years in order to qualify. Find an application here. https://renorodeo.com/get-involved/wranglers/.

Reno Rodeo. Photo by Rebecca Genesis

the rodeo. In Reno, everyone's a cowboy or cowgirl, during the rodeo's 10 days of magic. This family event has something to delight all ages: Xtreme bull riding, barrel racing, cattle roping, bronc busting, and, of course, the barrel men, or clowns. Even tots can get in on the action, as they take a turn at trying a special skill themselves. Mutton busting gives kids ages 4 to 7 a chance to see how long they can stay on the back of a sheep.

Author/artist Will James was paid $50 for creating the artwork for the 1919 cover for the souvenir program of the first annual Reno Round-Up.

AN ELEPHANT NAMED BERTHA

Who Was the Longest Running Casino Act in Nevada's History?

Celebrities are known to shave a few years off their ages while adding some to their birth years. Over time this adds to much confusion. Perhaps that is the intention. Like a lot of those showbiz sorts, there seems to be some discrepancy in the year of her birth.

For our purposes, I'm going with Bertha the elephant being born in the wilds of India in 1945. She was captured six years later.

When she was seventeen years old, Bertha was bought by John Ascuaga for $8000 at a Wisconsin Circus museum in 1962. For the next 37 years, she and the Nugget would become synonymous. Many saw her as the Nugget's unofficial mascot and that of the city of Sparks as well. Bertha was everywhere. Besides performing in the Nugget's Circus Room, she made appearances in local parades, including the annual Nevada Day parade and billboards. The Nugget bought two other smaller elephants to work with Bertha. The elephants were so popular in the community that the Nugget held a contest to name the other elephants.

The winning names were Tina and Angel. And while they worked with Bertha, it was understood she was the star. A special

---

CASINO WITH A LONG HISTORY

WHAT: The Nugget Hotel Casino

WHERE: 1100 Nugget Ave. Sparks, NV

COST: Costs vary depending on which restaurant you choose and whether or not you will gamble.

PRO TIP: This part of downtown Sparks has changed drastically since Bertha ruled the roost. The area where the elephant barn once stood is a parking lot today.

Nugget Showroom where Bertha performed (they brought her in through a side door)

elephant barn was built for Bertha, Tina, and Angel in the Nugget's back parking lot, and there they lived in comfort and style with their trainer, who had an apartment upstairs. As the years passed, Tina and Angel grew larger, outgrowing their roles in the elephant show. Once again, Bertha was a solo act at the Nugget.

The list of celebrities Bertha appeared with is endless. But if you're curious, a list of such stars would include Lucille Ball, Liberace, Lorne Green, Dan Blocker, and Tony Bennett. The beloved elephant also holds a record many could envy. She happens to be the longest-running casino act in Nevada history. Bertha was that popular. She, Tina, and Angel appeared on postcards and other items offered in the gift shop. Whiskey distiller Ezra Brooks even offered a Bertha decanter in 1970.

At age 53-54 on November 11, 1999, Bertha's passing was a sad day for everyone in Sparks, indeed for anyone who had ever met her. The pachyderm was a goodwill ambassador like no other, pulling in customers and friends from the moment of her arrival in 1962.

> Las Vegas has glitz, glamour, and mega-stars, but the Nugget is the only Nevada Casino ever to feature elephants.

DIVORCES AND DUDE RANCHES

Was Reno the "divorce capital of the world"?

At one time, Reno was Nevada's largest and most famous city. Reno was also the first Nevada city to attract the eyes and the pocketbooks of gamblers, movie stars, and all those unhappily married people seeking divorce. At one time, the Biggest Little City was considered the center of naughty nightlife. The city was also called the divorce capital of the world even though there were many more marriages performed in Reno than divorces. Regardless, divorce provided a nice little side hustle for local attorneys.

But there was one little problem, where would all these people live while meeting that six-week residency requirement? Reno enjoyed being seen as a western town. The astute encouraged the perception that everyone here wore jeans and 10-gallon hats. It worked for smart businessmen and businesswomen who saw an opportunity and created dude ranches with intriguing names for wealthy soon-to-be divorcees

REASONABLY PRICED RESIDENCES

WHAT: Riverside Artist Lofts

WHERE: 17 S Virginia St. (next door to the Washoe County Courthouse)

COST: Free to visit the floor level art gallery where residents showcase their work

PRO TIP: The Riverside Hotel was built in 1931 to provide a place for the deep pocketed divorce seeker to stay during his or her six-week residency. It's one of the few remaining such locations that catered to the divorce trade. In 2000, the hotel was converted to artist lofts so that local artists would have a reasonably priced apartment in which to create their art. Boxing great Jack Dempsey spent his six-week residency in a rented home at 761 California Ave. If you drive by, please don't disturb the residents.

The Eddy Riverside Artist Lofts

who would spend their required residency riding horses by day and club hopping by night.

They came for what they called the *cure*, or to be *renovated*. During the divorce boom, they contributed millions to Reno's economy.

Reno liked being ahead of the curve. It still does as a matter of fact.

> In 1956, playwright Arthur Miller spent his six weeks' residency at the divorce ranch at Pyramid Lake. During this time, he wrote *The Misfits*. When his divorce from Mary Slattery was final, Miller married Marilyn Monroe.

DYMAXION CAR

Where is a car you won't see every day?

The automobile world has always been filled with unusual cars. At the National Automobile Museum you can discover 200 such cars. There are cars like James Dean's 1949 Mercury Coupe, John Wayne's Corvette, and Frank Sinatra's Ghia. Aside from the 1907 Thomas Flyer that won the 1908 New York to Paris car race, there is the unique 1933 Dymaxion.

Rare as rare can be, that would be eccentric inventor Buckminster Fuller's 1933 Dymaxion car. Only three Dymaxions were ever made. The design was so startling that it was rumored to eventually be capable of flight. But alas, the design never caught on. Of course it didn't. There is nothing sleek or sensational about the Dymaxion car. It is ugly and clunky. Picture something between the Goodyear blimp and a vintage Volkswagen bus. But there is no denying that scarcity factor. Of the three there is no telling where two of them are.

But if you're anxious to gaze at this oddity you'll be happy to know that the remaining (or second prototype) Dymaxion car is right here in Reno at the National Automobile Museum. The museum was the creation of gambling magnate William Harrah who happened to be a car collector like no other. And some of his collection is included at the museum, so there are plenty of cars to see here. There is much to see and to learn at the National Automobile Museum. Be sure to check out Science Saturdays, a

DRIVEN TO SEE CARS

WHAT: National Automobile Museum

WHERE: 10 S Lake St.

COST: General admission is $12; seniors and children's tickets are less.

PRO TIP: You're within walking distance of the Reno Aces baseball stadium.

National Automobile Museum

hands on learning experience for the 8-12 year old set. But not to worry, adults are welcome to take part as well.

But you came especially for the rare Dymaxion car. Go ahead and look at it. Once you've seen this car, you're likely never to forget it. Now, aren't you glad they don't make 'em like they used to?

Buckminster Fuller was the inventor of the geodesic dome roof concept. A student of his, Don Richter, was co-owner of Temcor, which built the geodesic dome roof of the Pioneer Center for the Performing Arts.

THE MANSION THAT MOVED TWICE

When a house is moved, does the ghost go with it?

In 1877, local rancher W. J. Marsh built himself a fine home at the corner of S Virginia and California Avenue. Even before Marsh and his family moved into their new home, founder of Reno and local businessman, Myron Lake, coveted the house. In 1879, Marsh accepted Lake's offer to buy it for $5,000. If you're curious, that's roughly equivalent to $128,000 today. Good luck trying to buy a mansion for that in Reno today.

Although they owned the home, the Lake family would not live happily ever after in the Italianate-style mansion. In fact, Myron himself would never live there. Jane and Myron Lake divorced in 1881, and Myron died three years later. Eventually, Jane moved into the mansion and upgraded it with indoor plumbing and wall-to-wall carpeting. In 1902, she sold the home at a loss for $1,000. Myron was probably rolling in his grave, but it gets worse. A bank bought the property in the late 1960s with demolition in mind. Not so fast, said local historians who scrambled to get the money to have the mansion moved. In 1971, the Lake Mansion was moved two miles south to the grounds of the Reno-Sparks Convention Center. And there it would remain for 33 years—a historic oddity, out of place and out of time. Some claimed the place was haunted by the ghostly Jane Lake, who'd suddenly become possessive of her old home.

In 1871, hoping for Reno to become the county seat, Myron Lake donated the land that the courthouse was built upon.

Lake Mansion

With the coming of the 21st century, the Convention Center wanted to expand its parking lot. This meant something had to be done with the Lake Mansion, ghost and all, so it was given to Arts for All Nevada, and the mansion was moved for the second time in July 2004. It's just a few blocks north of its original location. Hopefully, 250 Court St. will be its final destination.

21ST CENTURY RETROFIT

WHAT: Lake Mansion

WHERE: 250 Court St. on the southeast corner of Court and Arlington Streets

COST: Free

PRO TIP: Self-guided tours are available Tuesday through Thursday from 1 to 4 p.m. Next door on Flint is the Pignic Pub & Patio. If you're hungry for something a bit different from the usual steak and burgers, check it out. Across Court St. is the Great Basin Community Food Co-Op, a healthy food source that offers locally grown and natural foods and juices.

RENO'S GREATEST UNSOLVED MYSTERY

Armchair detectives want to know—got any mysteries to solve?

Given the time that's passed, this one's likely never to be solved. March 22, 1934, 45-year-old Roy Frisch walked out the door of the home he shared with his mother and sisters, never to return. He was last seen walking south along Virginia St. where he stopped to talk to a friend. Did I mention that Frisch was set to testify against a couple of Reno's worst criminal elements, with gangster affiliations to Baby Face Nelson?

Searches were conducted, and rewards were offered. But there was no sign of Frisch. Did I also mention that Baby Face was in town at the time of Frisch's disappearance? And after Baby's untimely death in a gun battle with FBI agents, John Paul Chase, a cohort of Nelson's came forward with a confession. He and Baby Face killed Frisch and dumped his body in the Nevada desert. Chase being an inmate at Alcatraz, agreed to show authorities where Frisch was—if they would let him out of prison to do so.

They agreed, and off into the desert went guards and John Paul Chase. But the search turned up nothing. Chase couldn't remember

WHAT REALLY HAPPENED?

WHAT: Frisch Home

WHERE: 247 Court St., corner of Court and Arlington Streets

COST: Free to look at and photograph the building from the outside. Please don't disturb the tenants.

PRO TIP: You're a block south of the Reno Riverwalk along the Truckee River. Head north and stroll along the Riverwalk. You're also 0.3 miles north of the Nevada Museum of Art, the only accredited art museum in the state of Nevada. Look for the Burning Man art piece *Guardian of Eden* in front of the building.

Front door of Roy Frisch Home

exactly. The desert does look much the same, after all. Chase was taken back to Alcatraz, and the mystery of Roy Frisch's fate and his whereabouts continues.

Roy Frisch's family home is still there on the corner of Court and Arlington Streets (directly across the street from Lake Mansion). The family still owns it, although it's leased out to various businesses.

If you wish to retrace Frisch's last steps, start at the corner of First St. and Center St. Head west toward the Riverside lofts, turn right at the Truckee Riverwalk to Arlington, and turn left on Arlington, which will take you to the Frisch home. Roy never got this far.

At the time of his disappearance, Frisch worked at the Riverside Bank for George Wingfield, the wealthiest and most powerful man in Nevada and former owner of the Goldfield Hotel. Wingfield was being investigated for his dealings with Reno underworld figures William Graham and James McKay. Many believed Frisch's body was buried in the backyard of Wingfield's mansion, which was next door to the Frisch home. The mansion burned several years ago, and the Kimpton, a luxury 20-story hotel, is in the works for this location.

MARILYN'S LAST FILM

Was a cursed film made in Reno?

In her short career that spanned only 14 years, actress Marilyn Monroe appeared in 30 films. Because she didn't complete her last film *Something's Got to Give*, *The Misfits* is generally seen as her last film. Marilyn Monroe was the sexy blonde actress and purported lover of both JFK and his younger brother Robert.

Putting politicians and scandals aside, *The Misfits* was filmed right here in Reno. The screenplay was written by Arthur Miller, Marilyn's husband at the time. Because he was also working on the film, he accompanied Marilyn to Reno, which proved to be disastrous for the marriage. The Millers fought constantly. While Marilyn escaped into drugs, Miller apparently escaped into the loving arms of Inge Morath, a camera woman working on the film. And shortly after filming was completed, Miller divorced Marilyn and married Inge. This is one reason some have claimed the film was cursed.

The other reason the curse is talked about is the deaths. The film was Marilyn Monroe's last and that of her co-star Clark Gable as well. It was also the last for Nevada Lieutenant Governor Rex Bell who had a small part in the film. Cursed or not, *The Misfits* was a black-and-white box office flop almost from

---

NOTHING LASTS FOREVER

WHAT: Marilyn Monroe scene location from *The Misfits*

WHERE: Front door of the Washoe County Courthouse

COST: Free

PRO TIP: The front door is no longer used as an entrance, so photograph all you want. Ghost enthusiasts will tell you that Marilyn's ghost is said to visit this spot on occasion. Yes, I know she is in a crypt at the Westwood Cemetery in Los Angeles, but her ghost visits Reno.

Wedding Ring Bridge (right of photo is spot where Marilyn Monroe stood)

the moment it premiered. It remains a curiosity because it was Monroe and Gable's last film.

If you would like to see where Marilyn worked her magic, you can visit some of the filming locations, which included downtown Reno, outside the Washoe County Courthouse, inside the old Mapes Hotel (which has since been demolished), and outside at the wedding ring bridge (also demolished and replaced). The old Odeon Hall in nearby Dayton and Pyramid Lake are two other filming locations you might want to check out.

The present Washoe County Courthouse is the second at this location. The first was made of red brick, which still stands as an internal section of the present-day courthouse.

THE PROSPECTOR AT THE CHOCOLATE NUGGET CANDY FACTORY

What is the 18-foot-tall prospector panning for?

Chocolate! What else would he be looking for here at the Chocolate Nugget Candy Factory in Washoe Valley? The prospector started his career beckoning customers in front of the Claim Stake Casino in Sparks. When the failing casino was closed and that gig was behind him, the fiberglass prospector was relocated to the Chocolate Nugget Candy Factory here in Washoe Valley, and he's been here ever since. For those brave enough to take the short path out to where he sits, the prospector makes for a great photo op. Smile . . . it's just you and the prospector.

But it hasn't always been divinity and chocolate drops for the prospector. In the winter of 2017, the weight of a heavy snowstorm broke one of his arms. It's since been repaired and he's good as new.

SOMETHING SWEET

WHAT: Chocolate Nugget Factory

WHERE: 611 Hwy. 395 N., Washoe Valley

COST: Free to visit the prospector. The candy will cost you.

PRO TIP: You'll find lots of goodies here. The jalapeno peanut brittle is a specialty.

Some of the candy-making equipment in use at this family-run operation, such as the 1914 Fire Mixer, are antiques.

Cowpoke art at Chocolate Nugget Candy Factory

Legend has it the prospector was modeled after notorious southern Nevada gunfighter, prospector, and saloonkeeper Andrew Jackson (Jack) Longstreet. Since Longstreet died in 1928, long before the prospector came into being, we know he didn't pose for it, although he may have been recreated from a photo. Admittedly, there is some resemblance, but it could be nothing more than coincidence. Either way, the prospector and the candy store are there, just waiting for you.

RENO'S GENIE

What's more Americana than a genie hawking carpets?

Quick! Get a photo of fading Americana advertising—the Carpeteria's Genie of course. He won't grant you any wishes; nonetheless he is rare as the Genie who might. Progress has come, like it always does with innovative ideas and bulldozers, so that there are only a few of these tall Genies left. Luckily there are two in Nevada. There is one in Las Vegas and one in Southeast Reno on S Virginia St. The advertising icons were once synonymous with Carpeteria which was a big California and Nevada flooring business in the 1960s through the 90s. Back in the day, the living room of every modern home had a big leather recliner, two matching lamps, and wall-to-wall carpet was de rigueur.

But styles change, and so does everything else. Bigger businesses with bigger discounts

> ### MARKETING IS EVERYTHING
>
> **WHAT:** Carpeteria Genie
>
> **WHERE:** 8150 S Virginia St., Reno
>
> Take US 395/North-South Freeway Exit 61, and drive north two blocks. The genie is on the right.
>
> **COST:** Free—unless you're in the market for flooring. Then it's all up to you.
>
> **PRO TIP:** You're near fast food heaven with Burger King on one corner and In-N-Out on the other. If chicken's your thing, travel one block north for Pollo Loco.

Just a few decades ago, this area was considered far out of town. Today, with the 395 North and South on and off ramps, fast food, residential housing, hospitals, and schools, the genie has a much larger audience.

Genie stands tall outside of Carpeteria

came along pushing Carpeteria toward bankruptcy, although the franchised Reno store continues along on a smaller scale. As for the genie, he could stand a new coat of paint and is somewhat smaller than the other genies. Still, he continues grinning as he hoists a roll of carpet, all the while enticing motorists to stop and shop for flooring. There is no telling when progress will deem the genie useless and condemn him to an estate sale somewhere or, worse yet, the junk yard. So, smile now, because he won't be here forever.

THE BRÜKA THEATRE

Does Reno support performance art?

Yes, Reno is definitely a gambling town. More recently the Biggest Little City has become known as a college town—which it is of course. But Reno is a town that embraces the arts as well. All you need to do is come on in to the Brüka Theatre to discover that the performance arts are alive and well in Reno. The Brüka Theatre, located in downtown Reno, is community theater at its finest. Under the directorship of the multitalented Mary Bennett, the Brüka offers locals and visitors the chance to enjoy diverse performers in contemporary and classic plays, musicals, and theater for children.

There are two theaters within the Brüka Theatre building. The larger of the two is the street-level theater with its comfy sofa-style seating. The basement theater is smaller with just as comfy traditional theater seating. The bar is also located here, offering refreshments, a variety of soft drinks, water, and adult beverages.

A favorite Reno holiday staple and tradition is the Brüka's annual Buttcracker. It's not the Nutcracker—not even close. With apologies to Clara, there are those theatergoers who insist that Buttcracker is far more entertaining. It is the perfect mix of hilarity and parody. And it does serve to show just how much talent is involved in the Brüka Theatre.

BREAK A LEG

WHAT: Brüka Theatre

WHERE: 99 N Virginia St. (corner of N Virginia and First Streets in downtown Reno)

COST: Ticket prices vary from $20 and up for musicals (with discounts for artists and students). Children's tickets are $5 for plays and $10 for musicals.

PRO TIP: If you'd like to be part of the entertainment excitement of the Brüka, check out volunteer opportunities. Contact Holly Natwora 775-323-3221.

Brüka Theatre

    This is not one of those places you'll visit once and forget about. I guarantee that once you discover the Brüka, you'll be back again and again. Yes, this is what entertainment is all about.

> The building in which the Brüka is housed was a haberdashery at one time and is another of those buildings where a ghost is said to lurk. Those who've encountered the ghost say that he was connected to that shop.

BELIEVE IN BURNING MAN ART

Looking for a great photo op?

The Burning Man event takes place in the Black Rock Desert, a two-and-a-half hour drive from Reno. Yet, it is an event that Renoites know well. Known as burners, the people who attend Burning Man are either coming or going through Reno. They drive their dust covered vehicles through town in early September on their way home from Burning Man. Many of them arrive and leave town by jet. Before boarding, they kindly donate their dust covered bikes to local charity. Burners pump millions of dollars into the city's economy each year as they load up on essentials before driving out to the desert for the annual art festival known as Burning Man. Every Renoite knows not to go shopping just before or after Burning Man—the shelves will be bare.

STAND STILL AND SMILE

WHAT: City Plaza

WHERE: City Plaza corner of N Virginia and First Streets (across from the Brüka Theatre)

COST: Free to enjoy and photograph

PRO TIP: You're next door to (south of) Reno's historic 1933 post office, as well as the Basement, which offers the trendiest shopping, a coffee shop, and a barber shop.

The historic Mapes Hotel once stood on this lot from 1947 to 2000. The Mapes was closed in 1982 and remained boarded up until it was demolished in January 2000. It's the only building placed on the National Register of Historic Places that has been demolished.

BELIEVE

Much of the art created for the event finds its way to Reno where it is displayed for all to enjoy. Even the less brave souls who aren't willing to spend a week in the desert without all the comforts of home, can enjoy the art created for Burning Man.

The question is, do you believe? You might if you visit the City Plaza (the site of the former Mapes Hotel) across from Reno City Hall. This is where the *BELIEVE* sculpture is located. Created for the 2013 Burning Man by artists Jeff Schomberg and Laura Kimpton, the word "BELIEVE" is spelled out in 12-foot-high steel letters and is 70 feet across. The art displayed here brings a lively new vibe to the downtown area. Rio de Janeiro has its spectacular street art and Reno has its Burning Man art.

Politicians and everyone else seem to agree; on any given day, rain, snow, or shine, you will always find someone eagerly posing for a photo with *BELIEVE*.

THE EDDY

Where can an artist find a collaborative community?

Trendy is the key here. And with an innovative younger crowd re-discovering downtown Reno, something new and different is always happening. A good example of this is the Eddy, which follows the example of downtown Las Vegas' Container Park. Utilizing shipping containers is environmentally savvy. The Eddy in downtown Reno is a collaborative open-air space, comprised of three repurposed shipping container bars and food trucks. Unlike Las Vegas there aren't a lot of chi-chi shops at the Eddy. Instead, there is common area seating on the Riverwalk at the Truckee River.

When you're ready to eat, expect standard fare like pizza and tacos; there are no designer dishes here. This may not sound elegant enough for some diners. In that case, a short walk in either direction will have you at a place with a more gourmet friendly menu. But, if you are happy just to enjoy the ambiance of the Truckee River, local artwork, hand crafted cocktails, or craft beer the Eddy may just be your cup of tea—herbal perhaps. Of course, there is live music to enhance your dining and drinking experience.

If you're an artist know that the Eddy supports art and partners with local artists while being a fun spot where the community can gather, socialize, and enjoy the outdoors.

> **WINING AND DINING AT THE RIVER'S EDGE**
>
> **WHAT:** The Eddy
>
> **WHERE:** 16 S Sierra St. on the Riverwalk
>
> **COST:** Games and fitness classes are free. Prices for food, beers, and other drinks vary.
>
> **PRO TIP:** The Eddy is kid friendly and dog friendly during the day. At night, the dogs are still welcome, but it's adults 21 and over only.

The Eddy with the Riverside Artist Lofts

And if variety is the spice of your life, you'll be happy to know that there are no less than 24 craft beers on tap, cocktails, and 10 fine wines, as well. But no one lives by bread alone, think of the carbs. So, the Eddy offers classes. For the fit and the wanna-be-fit crowd there are free fitness classes and free games.

In this area on February 19, 1878, J. W. Rover was hanged for the murder of his partner I. N. Sharp on the edge of the Black Rock Desert. Eilley Bower, known as the Washoe Seeress, claimed that shortly after his execution, the ghostly Rover appeared before her at Bowers Mansion, proclaiming his innocence.

GALENA CREEK BRIDGE

Can you get a different perspective of the bridge?

As you look at the Galena Creek Bridge you'll be struck by the contrast between nature's beauty and that of man's engineering. It is an amazing sight. And for the record, the Galena Creek Bridge is the longest cathedral arch bridge in the world. The 295 feet high and 1,725 feet long bridge connects Reno to Carson City across Washoe Valley. With the population of the Reno area steadily increasing, old Hwy. 395 couldn't keep up with the demand. The area around Pleasant Valley and Washoe Valley was becoming congested with the steady stream of south and northbound traffic. On top of that, this is a wind prone area where winds can reach speeds fierce enough to topple large semi-trucks. In the winter this was an especially treacherous stretch of road.

Clearly an alternative was needed. When a bridge was first proposed, one of the major concerns for builders was the winds that swept across Washoe Valley. These concerns were still on the minds of everyone involved, when bridge construction began in 2003.

From the beginning there was a lot of controversy surrounding the project. At one point construction was stalled altogether. And one of the contractors backed out of the project. But after a number of safety issues were addressed and corrected a new contractor took over the construction in 2006 and in 2012 the bridge was open to traffic. The bridge has achieved its purpose of cutting down travel

---

> Because it took so long from start to finish, locals called Galena Creek Bridge the bridge to nowhere. It's also one of the most controversial and expensive projects in Nevada's history.

Galena Creek Bridge

NEVADA'S COSTLIEST

WHAT: View of Galena Creek Bridge

WHERE: Several spots along old Hwy. 395

COST: Free

PRO TIP: To get a closer view of the bridge, you'll need to go through the small community of Pleasant Valley.

time from Reno to Carson City, and alleviating traffic issues on old Hwy. 395. Those who live in Pleasant Valley can once again enjoy peace and quiet without the constant drone of busy highway traffic.

One thing motorists notice is that there is little sensation of traveling across a bridge on the Galena Creek Bridge. As with many other bridges, it's all but impossible to see the bridge's beauty while crossing it. To truly appreciate the bridge's design, you will have to put some distance between you and the bridge.

ORSON HYDE'S CURSE

Does anyone believe in curses?

Whenever unusual natural occurrences happen in the Washoe Valley area, the long dead Orson Hyde and his curse gets the blame. Ten years before Nevada achieved statehood, Mormon settler Orson Hyde was sent by church leader Brigham Young to the Carson Valley to serve as probate judge of Carson County in 1854.

One of the first things Hyde did was to change the name of the settlement from Mormon Station to Genoa, a name that stands to this day.

Three years later, fearing a war with the United States, Brigham Young called for all the faithful to return to Salt Lake. Orson Hyde packed up ready to obey. But In order to heed Young's call, it would be necessary for him to leave his sawmill and other land holdings behind. He had little time. In desperation, he struck a deal with Jacob Rose, who was to rent the property. When the morning of his departure came, Hyde reluctantly left the Carson Valley, still expecting that Jacob Rose would send the rent money he owed for the property.

After five years Orson Hyde had still not received payment. He tried to induce Jacob Rose to honor their agreement. To no avail, clearly Rose had no intention of paying him for his holdings. When he finally realized that there was nothing he could do, Hyde angrily placed a curse on all those living in the region. He sat

SCARRED BY MUDSLIDES

WHAT: Slide Mountain (named for the number of landslides that occur on the mountain)

WHERE: Mt. Rose Hwy. (SR 431)

COST: Free

PRO TIP: Slide Mountain Trail is about a mile in length and offers some stunning views of Reno and the surrounding area. The trail head is located approximately 12.5 miles up the Mt. Rose Hwy.

Area of Washoe Valley near Slide Mountain

down and wrote a letter threatening thunder, earthquakes, and floods, complete with pestilence and famine for the way he'd been treated. Most people laughed at Hyde's arrogance. And yet, every time severe weather struck the area they thought of Orson Hyde. So it was that the Washoe Valley flood of 1880 was blamed on Orson Hyde's curse as was the terrible mud slide a century later.

Genoa, as pronounced in Nevada, sounds like Balboa. It sounds nothing like the city of the same name in Italy.

STEAMBOAT HOT SPRINGS

When not writing for the *Territorial Enterprise*, how did Mark Twain relax?

The Steamboat Hot Springs is just south of Reno, and up until the late 1980s, you could still witness geysers and steam rising up from the earth. After the geothermal plant was built in 1986, the geysers and steam became a thing of the past.

Native Americans considered the hot springs a sacred place. But humorist/writer Mark Twain is credited with naming the hot springs. In 1863, Twain wrote, "From one spring the boiling water is ejected a foot or more by the infernal force at work below, and in the vicinity of all of them one can hear a constant rumbling and surging, somewhat resembling the noises peculiar to a steamboat in motion"—hence the name. The springs were thought to be restorative. Boxing champion Jack Dempsey

CHILLIN' IN A HOT TUB

WHAT: Steamboat Hot Springs

WHERE: 16010 S. Virginia St. (eastside of the highway)

COST: Free to see the historic marker. Prices for therapies depend on which you choose.

PRO TIP: This is the perfect spot to relax before heading up the hill (Geiger Grade) to Virginia City.

Nearby is what was known as Fish Springs, the location of the Kelsay House that was featured on the *Unsolved Mysteries* episode on January 23, 1991. The Kelsays told their story and presented a photo of the ghost they called Samuel that was taken in 1982. The house was demolished recently to make room for a wider road and new apartments.

The Healing Center and Spa at Steamboat Hot Springs

trained for an upcoming match here in 1932. And in 1940 one of the greatest racehorses of all time, Man o' War was brought to Steamboat Hot Springs after suffering severe injuries. Later that same year Man o' War would go on to win the Kentucky Derby.

Where once several mineral spas existed, today there is one at the location, Steamboat Springs Healing Center. It features an outdoor tub and shower, aromatherapy, and private mineral baths all meant for relaxation and healing, just the way Mark Twain and his contemporaries did back in the early days of Nevada's glorious silver boom.

PYRAMID LAKE WATER BABIES

What's in a legend?

There's something mystical about Pyramid Lake, the large saltwater lake in the middle of the Nevada desert, 42 miles north of Reno. There is also something a bit overwhelming about the 188.03-square-mile lake that forms the largest portion of what remains of the ancient Lake Lahontan inland sea that covered most of Nevada at one time.

Located on the Paiute Indian Reservation, Pyramid Lake offers great fishing, boating, and camping. While you're here, take a look around at the unusual rock formations. There is no denying that this is an eerie place. As you may have guessed, legends abound here. One of the most frightening is that of the Water Babies.

According to one Native American legend, the Water Babies are the restless spirits of babies that were unwanted by the tribe, so they were tossed into the lake and forgotten about. Their bodies may have drowned, but their spirits lived on, growing more vengeful with each passing day. Water Babies are said to be responsible for the unlucky fishermen who vanish on the lake each year. The bodies of those who drown here are seldom recovered. This, it's said, is the work of the Water Babies.

SALTY AS THE OCEAN

WHAT: Pyramid Lake

WHERE: 42 miles north of Reno (take the Pyramid Lake Hwy.)

COST: Free to visit, swim, and picnic on the beach during the day

PRO TIP: Always check in with the Ranger Station at 2500 Lakeview Dr. in Sutcliffe for information, lake conditions, and any restrictions.

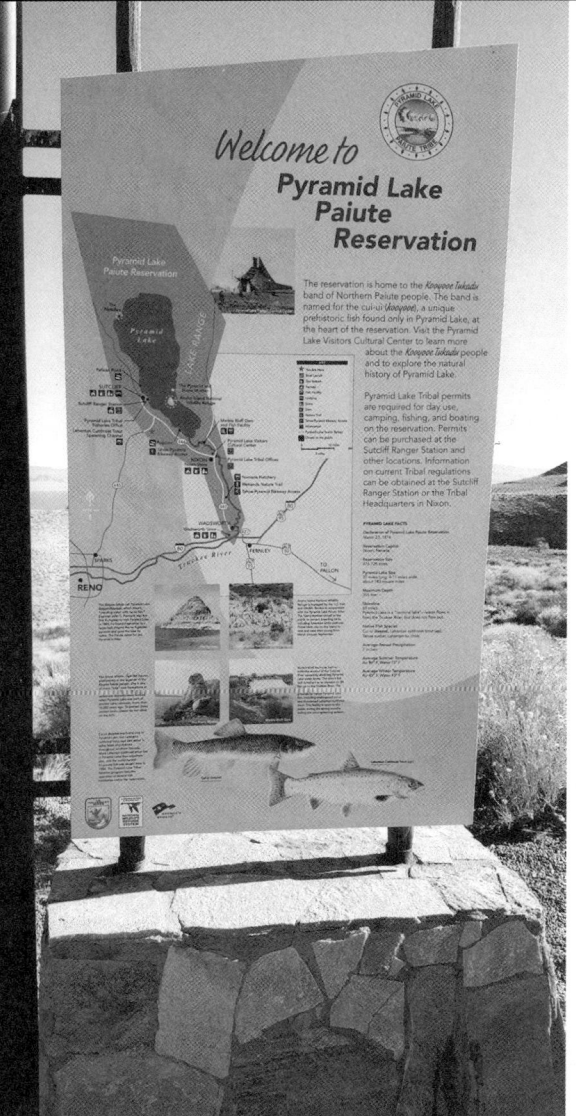

Pyramid Lake Sign

Not content to wreak havoc with boaters, the Water Babies also pull unsuspecting swimmers into the lake's murky depths, taking them to their doom. Even if you are only wading on the shore at dusk it is no guarantee you won't hear the child like cries of the Water Babies. Maybe it's just the wind playing tricks on you. Maybe the Water Babies are nothing more than legend.

During his 1844 exploration of the Great Basin, American explorer and unsuccessful presidential candidate, John C. Frémont, and his party encountered the Paiute people at their lake. Impressed with the pyramid-like tufa formations, Frémont called the lake Pyramid Lake.

JUDAS PRIEST: SUBLIMINAL MESSAGE TRIAL

What happens when heavy metal meets the judicial system?

The Washoe County Courthouse in downtown Reno has seen a lot of trials in its more than hundred-year history. None are stranger than the Judas Priest subliminal message trial that took place in the summer of 1990.

Two days before Christmas in 1985, 18-year-old Raymond Belknap and 19-year-old James Vance were smoking pot, drinking beer, and listening to the heavy metal band Judas Priest when they made their suicide pact. Belknap grabbed his sawed-off 12-gauge shotgun, and they walked to the playground of a local church. There they stepped onto the merry-go-round and rode it around. When it stopped, Belknap placed the gun under his chin and pulled the trigger. He died instantly. Vance picked up the shotgun. He would be next. But the bullet missed his brain, and he didn't die. Instead, he was horribly disfigured and would live another three years.

In 1990, Vance and Belknap's grieving parents brought civil suit against CBS Records and the Judas Priest band for $6.2 million, claiming the suicide and suicide attempt were the band's fault. The

LADY JUSTICE ISN'T TONE DEAF

WHAT: Washoe County Courthouse

WHERE: 117 S Virginia St.

COST: Free

PRO TIP: Once through the metal detector look for the painting of Myron Lake and the plaque dedicated to the two attorneys who lost their lives in the courthouse in 1960.

Washoe County Courthouse scene of the Judas Priest trial

contention was that their *Stained Class* album contained songs that had subliminal messages suggesting suicide: "Beyond the Realms of Death," "Heroes End," and their cover of Spooky Tooth's "Better By You, Better Than Me." The lyrics and the subliminal messaging, the plaintiffs said, drove the young men to suicide.

After both sides brought expert witnesses, Judas Priest was cleared of any wrongdoing on August 24, 1990.

Two murders occurred in a courtroom at the Washoe County Courthouse on November 23, 1960, during a contentious land dispute case. George (Sandman) Williams sneaked a gun into the courtroom; as the attorneys argued, Williams stood up, and shot and killed opposing counsel Eli Livierato and Edwin Mulcahy.

LINCOLN HIGHWAY BRIDGE RAILS

Has progress destroyed everything for the early days of travel?

When you're traveling down E Fourth St. in Reno, you may notice two things: this is not Reno's best side and there are a lot of motels. These are not gleaming new chain motels, these motels are old and small throwbacks from an earlier time when Fourth St. was a busy thoroughfare of cars traveling from east and west across the United States. Fourth St. was part of the Lincoln Highway, the early day transcontinental highway that linked the eastern part of the United States to the western part.

The Lincoln Highway was conceived in 1912 and dedicated a year later. With its completion, the United States was connected by a 3,389 mile highway that stretched from Times Square in New York to Lincoln Park in San Francisco.

Since the first wagon train came westward, the United States has been a nation of travelers. Now, travelers eager to see more of the country could do so. In their automobiles, they took to the Lincoln Highway that made its way through 13 states, including Utah, Nevada, and California. By 1927, the Lincoln Highway and

---

> In Nevada, the Lincoln Highway followed the original 1860 route of the pony express and the Overland Stage. Travelers along Nevada's Hwy. 50 (which parallels the old routes) are still traveling the same route. Markers along the highway point out the locations of pony express stations.

Lincoln Highway Bridge Rails

> **SAVING HISTORY**
>
> **WHAT:** Lincoln Highway Bridge Rails
>
> **WHERE:** I-80
>
> **COST:** Free
>
> **PRO TIP:** Getting here is tricky. You'll need to be traveling east on I-80. If you're going west, take the Verdi exit, and from there, get back on I-80 heading east.

Victory Highways were completed and converged in Reno. Reno businesspeople were thrilled with the opportunity. And now that travelers could drive to Reno, tourism flourished.

As more traffic came, the need for wider and safer highways increased. When progress came with its motor graders and wheel loaders, it looked as if the Lincoln Highway bridge rail sets were doomed. But luckily they were saved by the Nevada Department of Transportation and placed here at Mogul, six miles west of Reno, a reminder of how transcontinental travel once was in the early days of the 20th century.

PYRAMID LAKE: TWO LEGENDS AND A FISH

Why is the Cui-Ui so rare?

According to an ancient Paiute legend, Pyramid Lake is cursed by a mermaid who once lived in the lake. When she fell madly in love with a man from the village, the mermaid dreamed of being his wife, but his village had other ideas. They were all against the union and treated the mermaid shabbily. This made her so angry that she went back into the water, transformed herself into a monster serpent, and placed a curse upon the lake.

The unmistakable rock formation that resembles a hooded woman with her basket is called the Great Stone Mother by the Paiute. And according to legend, she was a young mother who lost her children, and then sat down and began to cry for them. She cried until her tears formed the lake. She continued crying until she herself turned to stone.

Anyone who's ever visited the lake knows there's no place like Pyramid Lake anywhere else on earth. Pyramid Lake is a world-class fishing destination,

---

GONE FISHING IN A PREHISTORIC LAKE

WHAT: Pyramid Lake

WHERE: 42 miles north of Reno (take the Pyramid Lake Hwy., and check in at the Ranger Station located at 2500 Lakeview Dr. in Sutcliffe)

COST: Free to visit, swim, and picnic on the beach during the day. While a Nevada fishing license isn't required, a Paiute Tribe permit is required for boating, fishing, and camping. Costs range from $12 per day to fish, $13 for boating, and $16 for camping.

PRO TIP: Sunbathers and picnickers should know there are no shade trees here, so bring your own umbrella. Overnight tent campers, be prepared for the predawn winds that can come whirling in out of nowhere.

Pyramid Lake

and the only place that can boast the cui-ui, which is an entire family of fish that is found nowhere else on earth. The two-million-year-old cui-ui, is a large sucker fish with a life span of 40 years, can grow to 27 inches in length, and can weigh up to 7 pounds. The cui-ui was a staple food source of the native Paiutes for hundreds of years. The cui-ui is being affected by climate and has been on the endangered list since 1967. There is a strict limit to the number of large fish you can have in your possession.

There is a theory that Lake Tahoe and Pyramid Lake are connected by a subterranean river system. This, they say, explains why the bodies of Pyramid Lake drowning victims have turned up in Lake Tahoe.

THAT TERRIBLE THANKSGIVING

Why are some people hesitant to walk in this area?

Reno will never forget Thanksgiving 1980. Downtown Reno was overrun with tourists set to enjoy a three-day weekend of gaming fun. The hotel/casinos that lined Virginia St. were ready to serve up traditional turkey dinners with all the trimmings. The sidewalks were teeming with people.

At a motel south of downtown, 51-year-old Priscilla Ford had other ideas. The voices in her head had told her that she must slaughter as many people as she could. After drinking half a bottle of whiskey, she crawled into her 1974 blue Lincoln Continental and drove toward downtown. She pulled the Continental onto the sidewalk beyond the Mapes Hotel and floored the gas pedal, plowing through the crowd. When she was finally stopped near the Reno Arch, 23 people lay maimed and bleeding and another seven were dead.

Priscilla Ford was convicted and sentenced to death. She would spend 25 years on Nevada's death row, appealing her conviction. She died of natural causes on January 28, 2005.

Many people still don't like walking on this section of the sidewalk on the east side of the arch. Some claim to experience

JUSTICE SLOW, BUT METHODICAL

WHAT: Scene of horrific crime

WHERE: Virginia St. (east side of the arch). Walk south from the former Harrah's site, now the new Reno City Center, to the Club Cal-Neva at the corner of 2nd St.

COST: Free

PRO TIP: If you're in the market to buy or sell, notice that you're within a few blocks of Reno's largest pawn shop, Palace Loan and Jewelry.

A downtown festival in the approximate area on Virignia St. where Priscilla Ford's horrific crime ended. Note the climbing wall on the left.

feelings of deep anxiety and sadness in this area. That's possible, according to paranormal experts who refer to this phenomenon as residual energy or place memory. Locations of great tragedy are imprinted with intense emotions, so that when someone who is sensitive comes along, the feelings are experienced anew.

After the downtown mass murder, Reno gambling was never the same. Not necessarily because of Ford's heinous crime, but because legalized gambling opened up across the country. Rather than come to Reno or Las Vegas, gamblers could find casinos closer to home.

LYNCHED FOR A MURDER THAT DIDN'T HAPPEN

What was the 601?

On this very spot overlooking the Truckee River on the evening of September 17, 1891, a lynching occurred in downtown Reno. A full moon hung in the sky as Luis Ortiz was brought here to die on the old iron bridge that once stood here.

It all started in July 1891 when Reno Constable Nash arrested Winnemucca ranch hand Luis Ortiz for being involved in a drunken brawl and for severely injuring three men in a knife fight. After Ortiz had sobered up in jail, Ortiz put him on a westbound train, with the warning not to return to Reno to cause trouble. History would have been very different had Luis Ortiz done as he was told. But he didn't. Instead, he came back to town two months later, ready to drink and have a good time.

Ortiz was a ranch hand who'd come to Reno and drank more than he could handle in the bar at the Grand Central Hotel (corner of Plaza and Virginia Streets). The more he drank, the rowdier he became. When Constable Nash tried to stop him from shooting up the saloon, Ortiz resisted. In the ensuing skirmish Nash was shot in the stomach.

The constable was taken to his doctor's home, and Ortiz was taken to the jail. The newspaper claimed Nash wasn't long for this earth, and this enraged the local vigilante group known as the 601. Made up of respectable men who hid their identities behind masks, the 601 kept the peace when no one else could or would.

They waited until late at night before coming to the jail and overpowering the guard.

The ghostly Luis Ortiz is said to walk a lonely path upon this bridge.

Original lamps from early bridge on the new bridge (in this vicinity Luis Ortiz was lynched)

STANDING ON HISTORY

WHAT: N Virginia St. bridge

WHERE: The bridge Ortiz was lynched on was replaced by the Wedding Ring Bridge in 1905, and that bridge has since been replaced by the new bridge.

COST: Free

PRO TIP: If you're on the west side of the bridge, you're at the edge of Reno's Riverwalk with its up-close views of the Truckee River and an occasional beaver.

"You're wanted downtown," one of them told Ortiz.

There was no mistaking what this mob had on its collective mind. They jostled the frightened man out of his cell and to the iron bridge. There they slipped the noose around his neck. "Have you any last request?"

"Water and a priest," Ortiz mumbled.

There was no water and certainly no priest. Ortiz was given a flask of whiskey. He took his last drink and was hoisted up on the bridge. Proud of their handiwork, they left Ortiz's body hanging there for several hours as a warning to passersby who might be thinking about engaging in gunplay.

A few days later, Constable Nash made a full recovery. No one was ever questioned or arrested for the murder of Louis Ortiz.

HAROLDS CLUB WAGON TRAIL MURAL

Where can you see something of Reno's gambling heritage?

Once as much a part of Reno as silver dollars and slot machines, the wagon trail mural that has graced the front of Harolds Club in downtown Reno for more than 40 years now hangs in front of the Reno Livestock Event Center. The steps it took to get the mural from downtown Reno to the Reno Livestock Event Center on Wells Ave. is something local preservationists are rightly proud of. The large 70- by 35-foot mural, consisting of 220 panels measuring 40 x 40 x 8 inches, was from a design concept by Theodore McFall of Pacific Grove, California. It was sculpted in metal and painted by renowned African American sculptor Sargent Claude Johnson of San Francisco. The Paine-Mahoney Company of Oakland finished the mural by firing the colors into its steel panels. Once completed, the mural was erected at Harolds Club in 1949 in homage to the old West. The words "dedicated in all humility to those who blazed the trail", appeared above the mural in red letters. The illusion of movement was created for the campfire and the waterfall through the use of lights in back of the sign. No one was thinking about the historical significance of the mural

---

AN EXAMPLE OF AFRICAN AMERICAN SCULPTOR SARGENT CLAUDE JOHNSON'S WORK

WHAT: Harolds Club Mural

WHERE: 1350 N Wells Ave. (Reno-Sparks Livestock Center)

COST: Free

PRO TIP: In the 1930s and 1940s, Reno's horse race track was located in this area. In 1932, boxing great Jack Dempsey sponsored Reno's Ride of Champions bucking horse event held here.

Harolds Club Mural

when Harrah's bought Harolds from Howard Hughes's corporation in 1995. The idea was expansion, which meant tearing down the Harolds building. At this point the mural's future looked grim. Apparently, the mural's time had passed. If a home couldn't be found for it, the mural could be headed to the scrapheap. It was placed in storage. Then, in 2007, a home was found for the mural. Today, it stands in front of the Reno-Sparks Livestock Event Center.

Harolds Club was family owned with Raymond "Pappy" Smith at the helm. Harolds was one of the first casinos in Reno to hire women blackjack dealers. The philanthropic Smith donated generously to the 1960s Olympic team and offered scholarships to help students get a college education.

WORLD'S TALLEST ARTIFICIAL CLIMBING WALL (page 14)

THE GAZEBO AT HUFFAKER MOUNTAIN (page 24)

WEDDING RING BRIDGE LEGEND (page 8)

ADAM UBER'S CURSE (page 172)

THE PROSPECTOR AT THE CHOCOLATE NUGGET CANDY FACTORY (page 56)

TORTOISE AND THE BOTTLE CAP GAZEBO (page 176)

SCHEELS FERRIS WHEEL, AQUARIUM, AND ARCADE (page 146)

A LITTLE RIVALRY (page 2)

SPARKS MARINA PARK (page 144)

PICON PUNCH AND POLTERGEISTS (page 156)

VIRGINIA LAKE (page 34)

THE BIGGEST LITTLE CITY IN THE WORLD (page 10)

SILVER BARON'S SILVER TEA SET (page 124)

THUNDER MOUNTAIN MONUMENT (page 180)

BELIEVE IN BURNING MAN ART (page 62)

OXBOW NATURE STUDY AREA

How can you get back to nature within a mile of downtown?

Unless you have school-age children in the house, you've probably not heard much about the Oxbow Nature Study Area. It is one of the Reno area's lesser-known locations for getting out and enjoying nature. Consequently, this is one of those places that locals, and thus tourists, often overlook. And this could be because the Oxbow Nature Study Area is located in a warehouse district and not the easiest place in Reno to find.

But don't let this fool you. This little gem is well worth it. And it is rarely crowded, if you visit at the right time. Best time is during the early mornings or early evening hours. If you decide to come out during late mornings on school days be prepared to see a parking lot full of school buses. These big yellow vehicles can mean only one thing; a throng of elementary school kids and their teachers. The Oxbow Nature Study Area offers a close opportunity for learning and is a hit with educators and their students.

A partnership between the Nevada Department of Wildlife and the City of Reno Parks Department, the Oxbow Nature Study Area is recognized by the US Fish and Wildlife Service as a national

---

> Oxbow is an interesting name that may have come from an oxbow bend of the Truckee River at the area, or it may have stemmed from the title of Virginia City author Walter Van Tilburg Clark's classic *Oxbow Incident*. Walter Van Tilburg Clark also wrote the classic *City of Trembling Leaves* that takes place in Reno.

Nature Study Area Walking Trail

A LAZY DAY OF EXPLORING

WHAT: Oxbow Nature Study Area (open year-round from 8 a.m. until sunset)

WHERE: 3100 Dickerson Rd.

COST: Free

PRO TIP: Leave your pets at home. Dogs and horses aren't permitted into the Oxbow Nature Study Area.

model for a successful urban nature center. It is small and covers only 22 acres. Yet it is home to an assortment of wildlife that includes mule deer, beavers, and Black crowned night herons.

The Oxbow Nature Study Area is a great place to bring the family for a little outdoor exploration, a picnic, or just a quick walk. If you're in for the walk, you should know that the walking trail covers about a mile, and the scenery is ever changing. As you go along you'll pass along grasslands, the Truckee River, and through a grove of cottonwood and willow trees.

It's hard to believe that you're within a mile of downtown Reno. And yet, you're back to nature's serenity, and all is quiet. Well, most of the time anyway; occasionally a train comes chugging down the track, reminding you that you really aren't out in the wilderness after all.

THE DEPOT

Where can you satisfy your craving for a good craft beer and a tasty hamburger?

Like many other Reno area buildings, this three story brick building was designed by Nevada architect Frederick DeLongchamps. It was built to serve as the depot for the Nevada-California-Oregon Railway. That was in 1910. Needless to say, plenty has changed since that time. Rather than demolishing a historical, sound building, it has been repurposed to become Reno's first brewery and distillery: The Depot. And it's become a mecca for beer connoisseurs and those who want to try Silver Corn Whiskey or other local spirits that start with grains milled on-site. Did I mention that the Silver Corn Whiskey was the gold medal winner of the 2015 San Francisco World Spirits Competition? If you want to take it with you, the

ARE YOU STILL HUNGRY?

WHAT: The Depot

WHERE: 325 E 4th St.

COST: Draft beer starts at $5 a glass. The hamburger will set you back the better part of a $20 bill.

PRO TIP: This building was designed by noted Nevada architect Frederic DeLongchamps, who designed many Reno buildings, including the Washoe County Courthouse.

The Nevada-California-Oregon Railway was a narrow-gauge railroad beset with problems from its inception. Cash flow was the biggest issue, but mismanagement wasn't far behind. Called the N-C-O, people began referring to it as the narrow, crooked, and ornery railroad.

The Depot

distillery sells beer and spirits by the bottle, the can, and, of course, the keg.

    Cocktails have names like Sparkle Pony, which is a nod to Burning Man and its unique lingo. A Sparkle Pony is someone who goes to Burning Man with lots of cute outfits but not enough survival gear.

    The décor is slick and polished, and except for the brick walls, nothing remains from the depot of yore. The food is better than your average pub grub. Now about that burger; they call it the Depot Melt, and it's sure to impress anyone who loves their burger with bacon and lots of it, onions, and Swiss cheese—you get the idea.

PLAY BALL...
BOCCE BALL

Is there a different ball game?

You're up for a ball game. But your softball team has lost—again. Golf is too frustrating, and bowling is not for you. So let's say you're tired of tennis and want to try something different. There's always Bocce Ball. If you haven't tried it yet, you owe it to yourself to step up and give it a try. Bocce Ball is not a new game. In fact, we could go all the way back to ancient times—5000 BC—to see Egyptians playing a similar game. Galileo is rumored to have played a form of bocce when he wasn't inventing things or gazing at the stars, that is. Closer to modern times, well sort of, George Washington built a bocce ball court at Mount Vernon in the 1780s.

So, bocce is an old game made new and exciting. You know what they say about everything old being new again. Thankfully, you won't have to travel too far to play the game. Bundox Bocce is located downtown and offers two indoor courts and seven outdoor courts. Bring a friend or 20+, and Bundox has you

---

The Renaissance was Newt Crumley's Holiday Hotel in the late 1950s and early 1960s. Before moving to Reno, Crumley owned the Commercial Hotel in Elko. And it was here that he started a Nevada tradition in the early 1940s. To keep customers in the casino and gambling longer, Crumley brought top name entertainers to perform. Reno and Las Vegas soon followed, and the rest is entertainment history.

Outside the Bocce Ball court at the Renaissance Reno Downtown Hotel

GOOD ENOUGH FOR GEORGE AND GALILEO

WHAT: Bocce ball

WHERE: 1 S Lake St. (at the Renaissance)

COST: $20 for 50 minutes of play time for two

PRO TIP: No reservations are taken, so it's first come, first served.

covered. After a game or two you probably will be hooked, just like Galileo and George Washington.

After you've won by throwing your ball closer to the pallino (jack) ball than your opponent, you may be hungry and thirsty. Not to worry, there's an array of treats and drinks on the menu. Children are welcome until 9 p.m., and then it's an adult-only venue.

THE SILVER DOLLAR SCANDAL

What was the Redfield Hoard?

LaVere Redfield was a Reno legend. Some Reno old-timers remember him as a man who dressed in overalls, old shirts, and work boots, and as a man who liked to gamble. Most people he encountered didn't know who he was or that he was a millionaire many times over with more money than he would ever need. No one knew about that safe stocked full of cash and jewelry that was stored in the basement of his stone mansion on Mt. Rose St.

Redfield didn't trust banks, and he didn't like paper money, so he insisted on being paid for his casino winnings and business deals in silver dollars. These he kept in cloth bags. In 1952, robbers went to his house, fed his dog a juicy bone, and then carted off a safe containing $1,500,000 in cash and jewelry. During their investigation, detectives discovered that Redfield had neglected to pay federal tax on his gambling winnings. That's a big no-no. He was convicted of tax evasion, paid a fine of $60,000, and served 18 months in prison.

At trial, one of those involved in the robbery of Redfield's mansion claimed she was Redfield's sweetheart, surely news to his wife, and that he had told her she could have the safe. This was more news for the wife.

IF THOSE WALLS COULD TALK

WHAT: The Redfield Mansion (a private residence)

WHERE: 370 Mt. Rose St.

COST: Free to drive by and photograph.

PRO TIP: Please respect the owner's privacy. You're a block west of Lakeside Dr. If you make a right at Lakeside, you'll be within blocks of Virginia Lake.

Redfield Mansion

One story has it that Redfield was on the cheap side of frugal. He preferred walking to downtown Reno from his home rather than driving his old Chevy pickup the few miles because he didn't want to spend money for gas.

When he died in 1974, his hoard of silver dollars was discovered in his basement. There were 680 bags of gold and silver coins. The bags weighed more than 11 tons and contained 407,283 Peace and Morgan Silver dollars, and most were uncirculated.

When you see silver dollars that are listed from the Redfield Hoard, now you know where they came from.

Rare indeed was the $1 bill in Nevada until the late 1970s. Silver dollar coins (clad or not) were known as cartwheels and were used exclusively until 1978 when Eisenhower dollar coins were no longer minted and issued.

SHAMROCKS FOR BILL BLANCHFIELD

Why shamrocks on a grave?

After World War I ended, Royal Flying Corps of Great Britain pilot, Bill Blanchfield immigrated to the United States and went to work for the US Mail Service as an airmail pilot. His run was the Reno to Elko. Flying a refitted World War I de Havilland, the intrepid young pilot flew out of Reno each day at 10 minutes to 8 in the morning and landed in Elko two and a half hours later. Like the previous century's pony express riders, the airmail pilots captured the public's imagination; these young aviators were faced with a new danger, one the pony express riders could not have even imagined. They were the 20th-century heroes.

Blanchfield's exploits as an aviator were legendary among Renoites who eagerly read about his adventures. The handsome Irishman racked up 709 hours and nearly 63,000 miles flying across the Nevada desert. His untimely death on August 1, 1924,

---

Bill Blanchfield's bi-plane crashed near the historic Hillside Cemetery and University of Nevada Reno. Hillside Cemetery was established in 1875, and is the oldest cemetery in Reno. There is much controversy surrounding the cemetery because of its proximity to the university campus. Developers want to disinter and develop. This has been done before in Reno at other locations. But this time, historians and preservationists hope to persevere.

Hillside Cemetery

A HERO LIES HERE

WHAT: Bill Blanchfield's Grave

WHERE: Mountain View Cemetery, 435 Stoker Ave.

COST: Free

PRO TIP: The cemetery doesn't allow photographs of graves without the consent of the plot owner or family.

during a flyover of a friend's outdoor funeral service left Reno devastated.

William F. Blanchfield was buried with full military honors in the Mountain View Cemetery on August 4, 1924. The Reno Air Field was renamed Blanchfield in his honor. The following St. Patrick's Day in 1925, a small package from County Cork, Ireland arrived at the office of the manager of the cemetery. Inside were a small mound of shamrocks and a note from Blanchfield's mother asking that they be placed upon her son's grave on Ireland's special day. The shamrocks were dutifully put on the pilot's grave.

Until her death, Mrs. Blanchfield continued to send shamrocks to adorn her son's grave on St. Patrick's Day. The tradition of placing shamrocks on Bill Blanchfield's grave has been a Reno tradition ever since.

STREET VIBRATIONS MOTORCYCLE SPRING AND FALL RALLY

Is there anything for motorcycle riders closer than Sturgis?

The road beckons. Whether you travel by car or motorcycle, getting out on the road is inviting. There is where our love of the automobile, in addition to our love of the motorcycle comes in. It doesn't really matter whether you ride a Harley-Davidson, another big motorcycle, or what type motorcycle you ride, or don't, this is what Street Vibrations is all about. The motorcycle event has been around since the early 1990s and is one of the Reno area's favorite events. Spring and fall, you'll know it's Street Vibrations when you hear the roar of motorcycles echoing across the region. Even if you're not a rider, you've got to admit that there's something exhilarating about gawking at all those expensively painted and chromed enhanced machines with their custom and extended handlebars.

> ## GOT YOUR LEATHERS?
>
> **WHAT:** Street Vibrations
>
> **WHERE:** Downtown Reno, Carson City, and Virginia City
>
> **COST:** Free to gaze at motorcycles. Food and other items vary in price.
>
> **PRO TIP:** Prepare for crowds. This is one of the area's most favorite events.

The three-day spring event takes place in June, while the fall rally in September is billed as the last rally of the season. Both events draw thousands of riders and enthusiasts to downtown Reno, Carson City, Virginia City, and Lake Tahoe.

They come for any number of reasons: the motorcycles, for the camaraderie, the ride, for the live entertainment, and

Street Vibrations Virginia City photo by Cindy Hunt

the vendor booths offering all manner of goodies from gear to photos. There are plenty of food and drink venues for those that get hungry and thirsty while looking over some awesome street machines.

Street Vibrations has grown since its early days and can now claim bragging rights to the fact that it is one of the four largest motorcycle events in the United States. Yes, if you're on the West Coast it's a lot closer than Sturgis.

> One of the favorite runs for motorcycle riders is to travel up Geiger Grade (Hwy. 341) to Virginia City. Hairpin turns and breathtaking views make for an exhilarating ride.

ZEBRAS, TIGERS, AND SHRUNKEN HEADS... OH MY!

Is there such thing as a real shrunken head?

When California implemented a state income tax in 1935 wealthy businessman Wilbur D. May decided to take his millions and leave the state. In Reno, May bought his own cattle ranch (Double Diamond Ranch) and added horse breeder to his many endeavors.

In addition to being a business man, May was also an adventurer, big game hunter, and pilot. And did I mention that he was also a collector and a philanthropist? And it is through his generosity that the Wilbur D. May Center came into being in 1985 at the Reno's San Rafael Regional Park.

The Wilbur D. May Center has an arboretum, and a botanical garden which combined cover over 13 acres. Take your time and wear comfortable shoes, but don't leave before checking out the museum. The museum offers both permanent collections and traveling exhibitions. It also contains many of May's private antiques and collectibles, like zebra skin rugs, Egyptian scarab figures, and big game trophies.

Say "Hi" to the giraffe and monkey overhead. The piece de résistance for those who like their objects de art on the most unusual

> **DID YOU SEE THAT?**
>
> **WHAT:** Wilbur D. May Center
>
> **WHERE:** Rancho San Rafael Regional Park, 1595 N Sierra St.
>
> **COST:** $6 for adults, $4 for seniors and for kids 3–17. Special events are more: $10 for adults and $9 for seniors and kids 3–17.
>
> **PRO TIP:** There is plenty of free parking; and the arboretum and the botanical garden are free to visit. Wear comfortable shoes. You'll do a lot of walking here.

Rancho San Rafael Regional Park

side is the shrunken head from South America. Yes it's real! Look close—this is what tribes did to their enemies. How did they do that? Let's leave the lurid details of just how this was achieved for another time. Meanwhile, there are the rare Tang Dynasty pottery from China and the Eskimo scrimshaws.

Rancho San Rafael Regional Park is also the location of Reno's annual Great Balloon Race.

LUCKY LINDY LANDS IN RENO ON SEPTEMBER 19, 1927

Did Reno play a part in US aviation history?

As a matter of fact, Reno did play a part in aviation history on Monday, September 19, 1927, when Charles Lindbergh came to town. It was warmer than usual in Reno. A crowd of more than 6,000 people waited at Blanchfield airfield in Southwest Reno for the arrival of Lucky Lindy, Charles Lindbergh. Cars were parked one next to the other. Police roped off a barricade in an attempt to hold the throng of fans back from their hero. Having been awarded the Congressional Medal of Honor from President Coolidge, as well as numerous other awards and medals, Lindbergh was indeed the man of the hour.

An eager crowd of children and adults scanned the clear blue sky anxiously. Everyone wanted to see the brave young man who had flown 3,500 miles nonstop across the Atlantic from Long Island in New York to Paris, setting a new flight record. The sun rose higher in the sky. At 1:40 p.m., the piloted plane was due to set down. A cheer

KEEP YOUR EYES SKYWARD

WHAT: Site where Lindbergh landed (today the Blanchfield airfield is the Washoe County Golf Course)

WHERE: 2601 Foley Way

COST: Free to look at the historic marker that was placed marking Reno's first airmail field (Plumas St.). Fee for a round of golf is from $30 to $50, depending on the time of day you choose to play.

PRO TIP: The hungry and thirsty may want to try The Shoe Bar & Grill located at the golf course. No membership is required to enjoy the bar and grill, and you'll get great food and views of the Reno skyline on the patio.

Plaque on rock commemorating Reno's early flight history

arose from the crowd. It wouldn't be long now. Minutes later, the *Spirit of St. Louis* slowly came into view from the west. The crowd went wild as the plane approached the Blanchfield airfield and circled high overhead. Swooping down over the field and then back up into the air, the plane circled the field for nearly 10 minutes before landing.

The crowd pushed through the barricade and raced to its hero. Lindbergh smiled shyly. He spoke to Mayor E. E. Roberts and other officials on hand. Later there would be a parade, and he would speak at Powning Park in downtown Reno; now he was tired and wanted only to rest. He and his entourage were driven to the Riverside Hotel where he would stay during his brief stop in Reno.

At the Steamboat Ditch Trail, there is a concrete directional arrow marker that was placed here to guide airmail pilots. A flashing beacon that was placed on a hilltop with the arrow has long disappeared.

TAKE HIM HOME TONIGHT

What's Reno's classic rock connection?

If Johnny Cash had actually shot a man in Reno just to watch him die, he would never have ended up in Folsom Prison. But that's poetic license and it works musically. There's music and then there's music. Some of the industry's biggest stars have come to Reno to perform, or to make music videos. Doug Supernaw's 1993 music video Reno was a hit within his genre of country/western, but Renoites, including then Mayor Pete Sferrazza didn't care for the song they thought uncomplimentary to the Biggest Little City in the World. It was even banned from at least one local radio station. But that's music and tastes vary.

In 1986 rocker Eddie Money came to Reno to shoot a music video. Later in his career Money would say that "Take Me Home Tonight" wasn't one of his favorites. Nonetheless the song was a hit.

"Take Me Home Tonight" from the album *Can't Hold Back* was released in August 1986 and captured the imagination of music lovers in the United States and around the world. The

> **WIN SOME . . . LOSE SOME**
>
> **WHAT:** Lawlor Events Center
> **WHERE:** 1664 N Virginia St.
> **COST:** Depends on the event
> **PRO TIP:** Both the Reno Historical Society and the Fleishmann Planetarium are within a block north on the same side of the street.

Lawlor Events Center is the largest such arena in northern Nevada. Other stars who have performed here include Fleetwood Mac, Tina Turner, Tom Petty, Santana, Cher, The Eagles, and Metallica.

Lawlor Events Center

song also led to a nomination in the Best Male Vocal in Rock Performance category for Money at the 29th Annual Grammy Awards. He may have lost out on that, but "Take Me Home Tonight" helped restore his career and that of Ronettes lead singer Ronnie Spector. Spector, who also appeared in the music video, sang part of her 1963 hit "Be My Baby" in "Take Me Home Tonight." The video featuring Eddie Money, Ronnie Spector, and that dangling microphone, was shot entirely in black and white and filmed right here in Reno at the empty Lawlor Events Center on the campus of the University of Nevada, Reno.

In 2007, 21 years after "Take Me Home Tonight," Eddie Money and the Ronettes were nominated into the music hall of fame. In homage to the late Eddie Money and his song, the Wolf Pack basketball team plays "Take Me Home Tonight" after each home game win at the Lawlor Events Center. With any luck UNR basketball fans will be hearing the song quite often.

DUCKS IN A ROW

Are yellow rubber duckies just for bathtubs?

In 2007 the Nevada Humane Society became a no-kill shelter and began the work to make all of Washoe County no-kill. This of course, was a costly proposition. More animals would need to be fed and sheltered indefinitely, or until suitable homes could be found for them. Since that time 100,000 animals have gone to their forever families and homes.

The Nevada Humane Society, which is the only open admission, no-kill shelter in the state of Nevada, receives no animal welfare funds from other agencies, including the Humane Society of the United States. So funding is crucial. The annual Duck Race helps provide funding so that the Nevada Humane Society can continue its vital work in caring for sick and homeless animals in the community.

Rain or shine, it happens in late August every year. The Nevada Humane Society's annual Duck Race and Festival benefits homeless animals in the community, and it's an event that pet-loving Renoites look forward to. On the day of the race, 20,000 yellow rubber duckies are dumped into the Truckee River downtown. Each has been numbered and adopted for $5 each. But if you're feeling particularly generous and lucky, you can buy the Quack Pack (5 duckies) for $20, the Quacker's Dozen (13 duckies) for $50, the Beak Bragada (25 duckies) for $90, or the Feathered Flotilla (50 duckies) for $175.

> ### QUACKING IT UP
>
> **WHAT:** The Duck Race and Festival
>
> **WHERE:** Wingfield Park in downtown Reno, 300 W First St.
>
> **COST:** Tickets are $5 each at the Nevada Humane Society, 2825 Longley Lane Suite B.
>
> **PRO TIP:** One caveat here: only Nevada residents may purchase a duck and thus a chance to win.

Photo courtesy of the Nevada Humane Society.

You've made your choice, and the ducks are in the water—let the race begin! Standing on the banks of the Truckee cheering your duck on probably doesn't do much good. But it's fun. If you're lucky enough to have your duck win the race and the grand prize, you'll have a choice, either $10,000 cash or a new car.

If you're not a winner, you don't get to take your ducky and go home. The ducks remain the property of the Nevada Humane Society. It's all in good fun. The duckies will swim another year giving everyone another chance to win. Meanwhile, you've helped provide the resources to take care of homeless animals in the Reno area for another year.

Originally called Belle Island, Wingfield Park was purchased by powerful and wealthy George Wingfield in 1920 when it became part of a bankruptcy. He donated it to the city of Reno, asking nothing in return. However, the Reno City Council was so grateful that they called it George Wingfield Park. Most of the name stuck.

SILVER BARON'S SILVER TEA SET

Are you sure this is how the silver barons lived?

Nevada isn't a state rich in resources, unless you count silver and gold. Then it's an entirely different story. Lucky for Nevadans, Renoites in particular, silver was discovered in nearby Virginia City. One of those miners who struck it rich and quickly moved up to silver baron status was John Mackay.

With all that wealth, a man should be married, so Mackay wasted no time in marrying the lovely Louise. Now Louise liked the finer things in life, you know all those things that silver could buy, and devoted husband Mackay saw it as his responsibility to indulge her cravings. He commissioned Tiffany & Company of New York to design and produce a magnificent tea set, complete with dinner and dessert service for the Mackays and 22 of their closest friends. The pieces were all of silver and all done by hand with 1,250 pieces in all. Victorian ostentation was a way of life for Mrs. Mackay in her Paris mansion. Just to make certain no one would ever have as grand a tea set as the Mrs., John Mackay bought the dies. There would be no copycat silver tea services.

But you know that old saying that you can't take it with you applied to the Mackays as well, and the family left a large, as in

---

John and Louise Mackay's granddaughter Ellin was the wife of composer Irving Berlin. She wrote four books, one of which was *The Silver Platter*. Published in 1957, *The Silver Platter* was the story of her grandmother Louise Mackay.

John Mackay statue in front of the Mackay Mines Building

ENRICHING LIVES

WHAT: Mackay Mines Building and W. M. Keck Earth Science and Mineral Engineering Museum on the University of Nevada, Reno, campus

WHERE: 1664 N Virginia St.

COST: Free

PRO TIP: Hours are Monday through Friday 9 a.m. to 4 p.m. This building is said to be haunted by at least two people.

really big, endowment to the University of Nevada, Reno, which is why we have the Mackay Mines Building and Mackay Stadium. And, yes, the silver tea set went to the university as well. It's at the W. M. Keck Earth Science and Mineral Engineering Museum on the University of Nevada, Reno, campus if you'd like to take a peek at it.

AT THE QUAD

What's Reno's connection to Mount Rushmore?

Not so fast. Once you've enjoyed the W. M. Keck Earth Science and Mineral Engineering Museum, step outside and notice the statue of John Mackay in front of the building. Mackay was one of the Bonanza Kings, the Big Four (four miners who became millionaires and important to their communities, thanks to Virginia City silver).

When he died in 1902, his widow Louise and his son wanted to do something for Nevada in his memory. In 1908, they commissioned sculptor Gutzom Borglum to create a statue of John Mackay. Borglum would later go on to fame as the sculptor of the four presidential faces at Mount Rushmore. After much debate as to where it would stand, the completed statue of Mackay was placed in front of the School of Mining at the quad. Mackay was down-to-earth and believed in hard work, thus the statue isn't in business attire

PASTORAL POMP AND CIRCUMSTANCE

WHAT: University of Nevada, Reno, campus

WHERE: 1664 N Virginia St.

COST: Free

PRO TIP: Check the schedule. Coming to the university during commencement or when another event is going on in the quad guarantees large crowds.

> The University of Nevada was founded in 1874 in Elko, Nevada. In 1885, the university was moved from Elko to Reno. University of Nevada, Reno, is home to Nevada's first medical school.

The Quad at UNR looking northward

but rather appears with sleeves rolled up, a pick in one hand, and a piece of ore in the other.

When weather permits, commencement is held at the quad with Mackay's statue visible to all. It was also seen in these movies: *Mother Is a Freshman* and *Mr. Belvedere Goes to College*. Lined by stately elm trees that are more than a century old, the quad is one of the oldest and most picturesque spots on the campus. Listed as a Jeffersonian Academic Village on the National Register of Historic Places, the quad follows Thomas Jefferson's design for the lawn at the University of Virginia.

JAMES D. HOFF PEACE OFFICER MEMORIAL

How are Nevada's peace officers honored in Reno?

Police work is fraught with danger, never more so than when an officer is working undercover. On the evening of June 25, 1979, 33-year-old Reno police officer James D. Hoff was murdered while working undercover in a drug sting gone terribly wrong. Unlike some larger cities, cop killings are a rare occurrence in Reno. In fact, Hoff's death marked 32 years since a police officer died in the line of duty. Hoff was the first Reno PD officer to be slain since 1947 when Captain Leroy Geach and Detective Sargeant Allan A. Glass were gunned down in a downtown hotel room by a teenaged killer.

The James D. Hoff Peace Officer Memorial at Idlewild Park that bears Hoff's name honors all of Nevada's fallen officers. Dedicated on October 22, 1988, the monument bears witness to

TRIBUTE TO THOSE WHO KEEP US SAFE

WHAT: James D. Hoff Peace Officer Memorial

WHERE: Idlewild Park, 1900 Idlewild Dr.

COST: Free

PRO TIP: Plan to spend an afternoon here. There are plenty of things to see and do at Idlewild Park, including the Rose Garden, the California Building, and kiddie land.

Peace officer is a term that encompasses both police officers and sheriff deputies. They are law enforcement whose jobs involve keeping the peace in their communities and risking their lives.

James D. Hoff Peace Officer Memorial

the dangers of being a peace officer. It's one way the community acknowledges and honors these brave men and women.

    The annual Nevada Law Enforcement Officer Memorial Ride takes place in the spring with a starting point at the memorial. Sponsored by the Blue Knights Nevada II law enforcement motorcycle club, the group ride to Virginia City is open to all bikes and classic cars with all proceeds going to the memorial.

LET THE GAMES BEGIN

Does Reno hold a Guinness World Record?

Setting a world record is a big deal here in the Biggest Little City in the World. On Saturday February 8, 2014, Reno was proud to see a new Guinness world record set at the Peppermill Hotel Casino. No, it wasn't set for the most buffet refills at one sitting, or the most cocktail waitresses singing Happy Birthday, or even the world's largest jackpot. While any of those aforementioned categories seem worthy of some sort of record attempt, this new world record was achieved by the most people playing checkers at one time.

That's right . . . 540 players gathered at the Peppermill and proceeded to set up their boards and their pieces to play Checkers. And in doing so, these players grabbed the world record for Reno. That is a lot of jumping and capturing.

Record or not, the highbrow among us may prefer the slower paced Chess, which is actually a newer game than Checkers. But, Checkers is one of the oldest games known to man. It is believed to have originated in Egypt around 1400 BC.

> **GAMBLING IS PART OF RENO'S CULTURE**
>
> **WHAT:** Peppermill Hotel Casino
>
> **WHERE:** 2707 S Virginia St.
>
> **COST:** Depends on what you're doing
>
> **PRO TIP:** This is adult fun; the kids probably won't enjoy it all that much.

The Peppermill Hotel Casino uses geothermal energy to heat all of its water. It's possibly the only green energy resort in the United States.

Peppermill Hotel Casino

In Merrie Olde England, the game is called draughts, but here in the United States, we know and love the game as checkers. And until someone somewhere else decides to gather more checker players playing simultaneously, the world record for checkers belongs to Reno. Now king me!

ATLAS ISN'T SHRUGGING

What sets Reno apart?

What is a city without its kitschy art? It's a city devoid of personality. And Reno certainly isn't without personality. As you make your way through the city, you'll notice a lot of traffic, a lot of stop lights, and a lot of kitschy offbeat art. Reno doesn't play favorites. The city embraces all art.

Some may argue that the gold colored Atlas statue in front of the European Fitness Center isn't really art at all, but rather something meant to convey the message of the business it represents. But art can represent anything, even offbeat attention grabbing art such as Atlas here. The statue has been here forever, if you count a bit more than 20 years as forever. Don't take Atlas for granted. The minute you get comfortable with him as he supports an open frame earth—he will be gone. In Greek mythology

> **PUMPING IRON IN THE SHADOW OF ATLAS**
>
> **WHAT:** European Fitness Center
>
> **WHERE:** 2999 S Virginia St. (next to the Peppermill)
>
> **COST:** Free to see and photograph Atlas
>
> **PRO TIP:** If you want a photo, park in the Peppermill parking lot, have lunch (or dinner), and walk the short distance to Atlas.

You've seen Atlas, now what? Major fun is about two and a half miles down South Virginia (on the same side of the street) at Magic Carpet Golf, the largest miniature golf course in Reno. Family owned and operated since 1974, the Magic Carpet is a Reno tradition with its giant tiki, a genie, dinosaurs, and more.

Atlas at European Health Spa

Zeus condemned Atlas to hold up the celestial heavens for all eternity, that's a lot more than 20 years.

Although it's certainly not as grand as the Atlas at Rockefeller Center in New York, this is Reno, and Reno is a one-of-a-kind city with one-of-a-kind art even if that art happens to be the "beauty is in the eye of the beholder" kind.

133

SHINE ON, RENO STAR

Is Reno an artsy town?

Every city has something that makes it unique. Hollywood has its Hollywood sign, St. Louis has its Gateway Arch, Paris has its Eiffel Tower, and Reno has its Star. Some may scoff at that comparison but let's not forget that in its early days the Eiffel Tower had its detractors. The Reno Star is one of those unusual art pieces that draw strong opinions. You will either love it, or hate it. There is no in between with the one-of-a-kind Reno Star.

Art, like beauty, is in the eye of the beholder. The Reno Star on the northwest corner of S McCarran Blvd. and S Virginia St. is one of those pieces of art that will have people scratching their heads, and asking the question, does that look like a star to you? No, but it did to the artists that created it. And isn't that what art is all about? It's a safe bet that, anyone traveling north on 395 for the first time will definitely wonder, just what on earth it is. It's been described as looking like giant pick up sticks or a sea anemone. Yes, the star is definitely different—an acquired taste if you will, one of those things you will probably come to love if you spend enough time waiting for the light to change at the corner of S Virginia and McCarran.

The Reno Star is a 10-foot base that contains 24 spears that are approximately 40 feet tall. When the star was first placed, the spears were bright red, but, more recently, they've been white. Whether or not they will remain this way is anyone's guess.

Created by lead artist Mark Szulgit and collaborating artist Brooke Z. Erdman, the Reno Star was created for the 2012 Burning Man and was gifted to Reno that same year. The sculpture bears a plaque that reads as follows in part:

Reno Star

The Reno Star celebrates the Great Basin Desert and the Nevada night sky. This landmark is a gift to the citizens of Reno.

Like it or hate it, the Reno Star is another example of Reno embracing public art, and that's a great thing for the city.

TWINKLE TWINKLE, WE DO WONDER WHAT YOU ARE

WHAT: The Reno Star

WHERE: Northwest corner of McCarran Blvd. and S Virginia St.

COST: Free

PRO TIP: This is one of Reno's busiest intersections. The best way to see the sculpture up close and personal is to park in nearby parking lots (across S Virginia St.) and walk to it.

This is yet another great piece of Burning Man art that is on display year-round in Reno.

MIDTOWN DISTRICT: A BOHEMIAN VIBE

Where do you shop when you're tired of the big department stores with the same lookalike merchandise?

Admit it. Sooner or later, you're going to grow weary of the big box cookie cutter department stores and what they have to offer. Even the most devout shopaholic can be overwhelmed by the sameness of merchandise from one store to the next. This also holds true of the one size fits all eateries and bars. When this happens, you don't need to make plans to visit the bay area. There's a place to go that is much closer to home.

It is Reno's shopping and dining district with a decidedly bohemian vibe—Midtown. Just like the bay area, Midtown is eclectic and diverse. Yet, it's within blocks of downtown Reno. The brainchild of several young entrepreneurs and artists, Midtown is one place you won't want to miss if your shopping excursions include getting something special for that someone special. What you'll find here are over 40 unique shopping locations, trendy clothing boutiques, a used record store, tattoo parlors, hardware stores, and the anchor, Junkee, with its antiques on one side of the building and clothing on the other side.

Let me just say that if you're looking for a special occasion ensemble or something different to wear, Junkee is the place. The outfitter of Burners (Burning Man attendees), this store has a bit of everything including the unusual. A caveat from one shopper

---

> Junkee, one of the largest stores in Midtown, is housed in the historic Shoshone Coca-Cola Bottling Company building that was built in 1927.

Photos by Bill Oberding.

ASSERT YOUR INDIVIDUALITY

WHAT: Midtown

WHERE: Midtown is several blocks along S Virginia St. from Mt. Rose to downtown Reno.

COST: Free to walk the sidewalks and window shop. Dining, drinking, and shopping is at your discretion.

PRO TIP: This should be your first stop when looking to buy something unusual.

to another—merchandise is always changing. If you see something you like today, buy it. Don't leave the store to think about it, only to return an hour later and find it gone.

When shopping makes you hungry there are over 20 eateries and bars including a pizzeria, to choose from including Great Full Gardens with its paleo, vegan, and soy free food choices. All its tasty soups are made from scratch and all are vegan. Paleo and plant-based dining at its finest. For the adult after dark crowd there is nightlife here as well—bars and wine bars. Death and Taxes even offers classes on bartending techniques, pairings, and homemade syrups.

THE COUNT AND THE COUNTESS

How far can you see on a clear day?

Don't think that Countess Angela Dandini wasn't a success in her own right before she married Count Alessandro Dandini di Cessena—because she was. Born a contessa, she was an internationally known fashion designer who owned Contessa Originals, a dress shop in downtown Reno that specialized in original design clothing.

She enjoyed friends in high places. The wedding ceremony for her second marriage took place in the Nevada governor's mansion with Governor Grant Sawyer and his wife Betty in attendance. The marriage didn't last two months.

The Count didn't have all the trappings of royalty. What he had done was make readers the world over happy with his invention of the three-way light bulb.

After an unhappy first marriage, Count Alessandro Dandini came to Reno where he taught classes in engineering at the University of Nevada, Reno. In Reno, he filed for and received a divorce from his first wife, and quickly remarried. Fourteen years after his second wife died, the Count met and married Angela Desideri, and together they helped make Reno history through their philanthropy.

It's no accident that the main campus of Truckee Meadows Community College is known as the Dandini Campus. The Count

> **PERFECT PICNIC SPOT**
>
> **WHAT:** Countess Angela Dandini Garden
> **WHERE:** 7000 Dandini Blvd.
> **COST:** Free
> **PRO TIP:** Even when you know exactly where you're going the garden can be tricky to find. It's directly across the campus from the soccer field and worth the trouble to see a nice view of Reno.

Countess Dandini Garden

and Countess purchased the land so that a community college and the Desert Research Institute (DRI) could be built. The DRI has been studying environmental issues since the 1960s. It's adjacent to the Dandini Campus, and sandwiched between the two is the Countess Angela Dandini Garden. There are benches and picnic tables you can sit on. On a clear day, you won't be able to see forever, but you can see miles out into Reno from the Countess Angela Dandini Garden.

> The Desert Research Institute has projects on all seven continents. In 2005, DRI scientists helped Chinese researchers in their quest to preserve the ancient terra cotta soldiers that were threatened by pollution.

THE GALVESTON GIANT TROUNCES THE GREAT WHITE HOPE

Why was novelist Jack London in Reno on July 4, 1910?

July is the hottest month of the year in Reno. On July 4, 1910, it was about to get a whole lot hotter. More than 30,000 people were in town for the fight that was being billed as the "Fight of the Century": Reigning heavyweight champion John Arthur (Jack) Johnson versus James (Jim) Jeffries. Jeffries, a former champion, had come out of retirement and wanted his title back. In a bit of wishful thinking, gamblers bet on Jeffries; in 10-7 odds, he was the odds-on favorite. Much to the chagrin of racists, and like boxing champion Muhammad Ali, who would come six decades later, Johnson loved the spotlight. The more he talked, the angrier racists got.

In an effort to prevent violence, Sheriff C. P. Ferrel decreed there would be no guns, no weapons, and no alcohol anywhere near the arena. More than 22,000 people squeezed into the

---

Reno's Sheriff C. P. Ferrel was an innovator who implemented reading lessons for illiterate Reno jail inmates. In 1911, he was involved with the Battle of Kelly Creek (the Last Massacre), Nevada's last recorded conflict between Indians and settlers near Winnemucca. Although Ferrel oversaw the investigation, he wasn't involved with the battle. He trailed members of Shoshone Mike's gang several days before capturing four and bringing them to Reno.

Historic Marker commemorating the historic fight between Johnson and Jefferies

> ### JACK JOHNSON MADE HISTORY HERE
>
> **WHAT:** Historic Marker
>
> **WHERE:** Southeast corner of Toano and Fourth Streets
>
> **COST:** Free
>
> **PRO TIP:** This is worth seeing for historic fight fans. While here, you might want to travel east on Fourth St. a few blocks for the historic Reno mainstay, Casales Halfway Club at 2501 E Fourth St. for homemade ravioli, spaghetti, and pizza. It may not be fancy, but you'll enjoy great Italian food at one of Nevada's oldest restaurants.

makeshift outdoor arena to watch the fight. Among them was novelist Jack London (Call of the Wild), who was in Reno to write about the fight for the *New York Herald*. In the newspapers on June 24, 1910, London wrote the following.

> *They are here to witness two strong men, hearty and husky, who will not kill each other but who will attempt, by skill and wit and gameness and endurance, to outdo each other in a sport that calls to the uttermost for the exercise of all these faculties.*

As badly as he wanted to win, Jeffries was no match for Johnson. After 15 rounds, his trainers threw in the towel, and Jack Johnson walked away the winner, to the astonishment of sportswriters everywhere.

141

SKYJACKER

What put Reno on the national news the night before Thanksgiving of 1971?

It's been 50 years. Even if he survived his leap into darkness, chances are that D. B. Cooper is long dead. Chances are that he didn't survive that jump, and ended up as a ragged pile of bones buried beneath years of growth with all that money in the mountainous region somewhere between Reno and Seattle. Then again, who wrote those taunting letters to the *Nevada State Journal* and the *Reno Evening Gazette*? One letter read: "Attention! Thanks for the hospitality. Was in a rut. D. B. Cooper."

Did Cooper himself send the letter to the FBI? Or did someone see the opportunity to add a plot twist to the greatest aviation mystery since Amelia Earhart vanished in the South Pacific? When the FBI closed the case in July 2016 on one of its longest-running mysteries, there were still no answers.

It started off in Portland when a man using the alias Cooper hijacked a Boeing 727 on the day before Thanksgiving, November 24, 1971. Telling flight attendants he had a bomb and he wanted four parachutes and $200,000 cash, D. B. Cooper's crime began. The plane landed in Seattle, and its passengers were permitted to deplane, leaving only a small flight crew onboard with the skyjacker. Cooper was given the cash and the parachutes,

STARTING POINT

WHAT: Reno International Airport

WHERE: 2001 Plumb Ln.

COST: Free

PRO TIP: Except for the general location, there's nothing left to see of this historic event. You're within minutes (a straight shot down Terminal Way [traveling north]) of the Grand Sierra Resort (GSR) at 2500 E Second St. where the new Breakthrough Reno (escape room) is located.

Front sign at Reno Tahoe International Airport

and the plane flew off into the stormy night skies. Its destination, as demanded by Cooper, was Mexico City.

The crew convinced Cooper that the plane would have to stop and refuel and when the plane touched down in Reno, Cooper was nowhere to be seen. He'd jumped somewhere between Seattle and Reno, taking the cash and the parachutes with him. After all the songs, the jokes, and the theories, the question concerning D. B. Cooper remains: Did he make it?

A thorough search was made of the plane and the area around the airport—nothing was found. The rattled flight crew spent the night at the Mapes Hotel in downtown Reno, and D. B. Cooper slipped into hijacking history. The case was officially closed on July 12, 2016. It remains the FBI's only unsolved hijacking case.

SPARKS MARINA PARK

How can you picnic and barbecue on the coast while in the desert?

The Sparks Marina Park is located on a site that was the Helms Construction Company's 100 feet deep gravel pit, from 1968 to 1995. In 1987 a massive leakage of solvents and other chemicals was discovered seeping into the pit. Because of this hazardous material the site was declared a superfund site, which meant the federal government would fund the mandatory and extensive cleanup. Nine years later with the cleanup completed, Helms gave the land to the city of Sparks. Plans were altered with the 1996 winter storm that swept into the area causing major flooding in Reno and Sparks. The flood waters filled the gravel pit and the Sparks Marina Park with its manmade lake was created.

Today you can imagine this . . . you're inland, a good 500 miles from the nearest coast, in the middle of the arid Great Basin and yet—you can't help but feel that you're somewhere near the canals of Venice, California. You're at the Sparks Marina with its approximately 70-acre manmade lake, in which people swim, fish, sail, scuba, and paddle board. The walking trail is more than a mile and encircles the marina. On sunny days, it's not unusual to see the area crowded with sunbathers and walkers alike.

Pack a picnic or bring your barbecue gear (gas only, no charcoal), and it's almost like being on the coast minus the waves. If you dream of hooking the big one, be sure and bring your fishing

---

For many years, this area was known as the Helms Gravel Pit. But all that changed with the 1997 flood that filled the pit with water, helping to create the Marina Park Lake. Put this under the lemons to lemonade category.

Lake at the Sparks Marina

LEMONS TO LEMONADE

WHAT: Sparks Marina Park

WHERE: 300 Howard Dr., Sparks

COST: Free to spend the day picnicking and walking

PRO TIP: Fishing license required to fish the Sparks Marina Lake. The cost of a fishing license will vary depending on if you're a Nevada resident or not, and if you're a senior (over 65 years of age). A one-day permit for residents is $9. Double that if you're a non-Nevada resident. For more information and to buy a license, check with the State of Nevada Division of Wildlife at 1100 Valley Rd., Reno 89512 (775-688-1500).

gear. There is a lot of shoreline to fish, so you might just catch a nice size rainbow trout or any other type of fish that's been introduced to the lake. Walk the trail around the marina and you'll see the resemblance to Venice with townhomes that face the water. You'll also note that you're within walking distance to the Legends Mall with its shopping. If you didn't bring that picnic and you're hungry, don't worry because there are plenty of good restaurants at the mall. You can also catch the latest movie at the luxury IMAX Galaxy Theatres with comfy lounge seats and a snack bar that offers wine as well as soft drinks. What wine pairs with extra buttery popcorn, would it be Chardonnay or Cabernet Sauvignon?

SCHEELS FERRIS WHEEL, AQUARIUM, AND ARCADE

Where can you go on a dreary day?

Reno doesn't get a lot of rain: 50 days a year on average or 7.39 inches annually. However, if it should be raining and you're looking for entertainment, head to Scheels. There's a lot to see and do here.

Any day's a great day to ride the Ferris wheel at Scheels, but a rainy day is perfect. The Ferris wheel is located inside the store, and at 65 feet tall, it certainly isn't the largest in the world. That happens to be the High Roller in Las Vegas at 550 feet. Even so, both Ferris wheels share a Silver State connection. Nevadan George Washington Gale Ferris Jr. invented the Ferris wheel in 1893.

It's raining and you're enjoying a ride on the Scheels Ferris wheel while a desert rainstorm soaks the thirsty city. What's more the ride only cost a dollar per person, and that's

SHOPPING
ENJOYMENT

WHAT: The Ferris wheel at Scheels

WHERE: 1200 Scheels Dr. (Legends Mall), Sparks

COST: Free to look around at the aquarium and other displays. $1 to ride the Ferris wheel.

PRO TIP: There is much to see and do at Legends Mall, including an IMAX Theater, restaurants, fast food, and shopping.

George Washington Gale Ferris Jr. died broke and alone in Pittsburgh in 1896 at the age of 37. The Ferris family home is located at 311 Third St. in Carson City. The house is currently being used as office space.

The aquarium and the Ferris wheel at Scheels

a bargain. But don't leave just yet. After the ride, you might take a look at Scheels two large 16,000-gallon aquariums. One is for freshwater fish, and the other is for those of the saltwater variety. If it's a Thursday, you can watch as scuba divers clean the aquarium and feed the fish. Take a look at the informative displays about the history of the Ferris wheel and the history of jeans.

Gamers, you're covered too. Arcade games and shooting simulators will keep you busy with classics such as Pac-Man or Cruis'n USA and an array of newer games.

With so much fun to be had, it's easy to forget that Scheels is a large sporting goods store—until you start looking around.

BAT BRIDGE (MCCARRAN BRIDGE)

Where's a fun place to view wildlife in Sparks?

There is nightlife and there is wildlife. This site is the best of both worlds, nocturnal wildlife. It is one of those locations that isn't the easiest to get to. It's also one that you almost have to see to believe. Bat Bridge (McCarran Bridge) is the spot for watching a large colony of bats. Contrary to what you've seen in the movies, bats don't always live in caves. Especially if they happen to be one of the 40,000 or so Brazilian free tail bats (Tadarida brasiliensis, if we must be technical) that lives under the bridge. Of all the things you might expect to see living just under a major thoroughfare in a busy 24/7 city, bats are probably the last. But apparently, and for whatever reason, the bridge beats a cave all the way around. By offering the ideal living condition for the bats, the bridge has become their new hangout.

These creatures will come out when they're good and ready.

ARE THEY HERE YET?

WHAT: McCarran Bridge

WHERE: West side of McCarran Blvd., just north of McCarran and Mill Streets

COST: Free

PRO TIP: Because there's no parking on the bridge, you'll need to park in the lot of a local business and walk.

An old Reno saying goes something like this—Reno is so close to Hell, you can see Sparks. And you might feel this way if you're not wearing mosquito repellant.

A bat's eye view of the Truckee River at McCarran Bridge

So, you'll just have to wait for it! As the sun slips behind the Sierras to the west, the nocturnal creatures come out of hiding en masse. You can put all thoughts of Bela Lugosi away; there are no capes and fangs. Nonetheless these little guys are fast and hungry. Reaching ground speeds of almost a hundred miles an hour, this little colony of bats will catch more than 100 tons of insects in a single night. This may not bode well for the insect population, but it is the way the food chain works.

As the bats move off in the distance you can't help but wonder just what *Dracula* author Bram Stoker might have made of Bat Bridge.

THE VOLKSWAGEN BUG

Is it a spider–or is it a bug?

With a Volkswagen body and six spindly legs, the bug, also known as the spider bug (albeit it is two legs short of the normal spidery eight), was created by artist David Fambrough who donated it to the city that designated it as public art. The bug sat atop an old fire station that was later repurposed as a homeless shelter. Because of the bug on its roof, people began calling the shelter the bug house.

Clearly the bug had its fans, and soon it became one of Reno's icons. Every Renoite knew and loved the bug. There seemed to be a rosy future for the bug. But everything changed in 2008; the building the bug perched on was sold. Even though the bug was Reno's first piece of public art, the new owner was not impressed and wanted no part of it. Its rosy future crumbling, things were beginning to look grim for the spider bug. The city offered the bug back to Fambrough with the suggestion he offer it to Scudder's Performance in Sparks.

DON'T BUG ME

WHAT: Spider Bug

WHERE: Scudder's Performance, 630 Victorian Ave., Sparks

COST: Free unless you need some work done on your car

PRO TIP: You're two minutes (0.1 mile to be exact), away from the best burger in Sparks, the In-N-Out Burger at 280 Pyramid Way.

Victorian Avenue, once known as B Street, achieved a listing in *Ripley's Believe It or Not* for being the longest single-sided street in the United States.

The Bug atop Scudder's

Renoites know how quickly something can be scrapped and demolished when it no longer fits in. Fans of the bug, crossed their fingers (this is Reno after all) and awaited its fate. Would the spider bug be dispatched to the scrap heap? Was this the end?

Not this time. Luck was with the bug. The owner of Scudder's Performance, a longtime admirer, said no way to the spider bug's trip to the junkyard. He agreed to take the bug to his roof. And with a little help from the community the bug was moved to the top of Scudder's Performance at 630 Victorian Ave. in Sparks in 2015. It was a big deal. The news media was on hand and the mayor came out for a ribbon cutting ceremony and citizens gathered to welcome the spider bug to its new, and hopefully forever, home in Sparks. And there the spider bug sits, across the street from Last Chance Joe. And here the bug exists, happily ever after. It's looking like Sparks is quickly becoming the city of second chances.

LAST CHANCE JOE

Who is the most famous icon in Sparks?

Most people would say that Last Chance Joe is Sparks' most famous icon. And yet, Joe isn't a singer, a dancer, a movie star, or a sports figure. Nonetheless, he is known and beloved far and wide. And his story proves that nothing lasts forever. No matter how historians and preservationists might struggle with the issue, Nevada is a state in which obsolescence comes fast. Last Chance Joe is but one example. The 36-foot-tall Joe stemmed from a design created by Roscoe Duke Reading, and used by the Nugget in its earlier promotions. Created in Hollywood by three companies, Joe was built in three sections. When completed, the three sections were shipped to Reno on a flatbed railcar and re-assembled by Reno Iron Works.

So, Last Chance Joe was to stand in front of John Ascuaga's Nugget from 1958, welcoming customers who yearned to pose with him. The white bearded, happy faced Joe represented mining, gambling, and good times in a homespun sort of way. It worked for John Ascuaga's family run, Nugget casino. With the endearing Joe at the front door, people were sure to come through that door.

During Christmas season 1969 the Nugget got in the spirit by having Joe decked out as Santa. Joe was the Nugget. And the Nugget was Joe. That news was reported by the *Reno Gazette Journal*. A nice story—and it was a bit of free advertising for the Nugget. But big changes were on the horizon for the casino and for Joe.

> Sparks was once called Harriman in honor of a railroad magnate. But city fathers (and mothers) decided to rechristen their tiny town Sparks, in honor of Governor John T. Sparks. Besides that, there was already a Harriman in New York.

Last Chance Joe in front of the Sparks Museum and Cultural Center

DO YOU KNOW JOE?

WHAT: Sparks Museum and Cultural Center

WHERE: 820 Victorian Ave., Sparks

COST: Free

PRO TIP: Depending on the time of year, there are many events and festivals held in this area of Victorian Avenue.

After decades in the gaming industry, John Ascuaga sold the Nugget to Global Gaming and Hospitality in 2014. The new owners weren't pleased with Joe and what he represented. They wanted something a bit more hip at their front door. The rustic Joe and his outdated mien would have to go. Times change, and the gap-toothed Joe simply wasn't sleek and sophisticated enough.

But not to worry, they would gladly agree to move Joe, provided it cost them nada. After much scrambling and the generous anonymous donations, Joe was moved right down the block to the Sparks Museum and Cultural Center. Time had not been kind; Joe was in bad shape. Restoring him to his former self would be a costly endeavor. But thanks to the generosity of those who loved Joe, donations poured in. Restoration began and with a new coat of paint, Joe's good to go once more.

CAMEL AND OSTRICH RACES

Which camel is better to ride, the Bactrian or dromedary?

Virginia City is one of eight national historic landmarks in Nevada, and it's right up the hill from Reno—about 20 miles, give or take. Mark Twain got his literary start here in Virginia City. From that time to now, Virginia City has offered offbeat fun. Come fall, and it's time for the International Camel and Ostrich Races, one of Virginia City's premier fun events. Imagine riders hanging on while dromedary camels race each other. Imagine a rider in a little cart as he or she tries to steer an ostrich toward the finish line. It all started with a tall tale. On a slow news day in 1960, Bob Richards, editor of Virginia City's *Territorial Enterprise*, wrote an article challenging other newspapers to come and race in the town's upcoming Labor Day camel races. The challenge backfired.

The *San Francisco Chronicle* accepted, sending camels to Virginia City. It just so happened that the film crew from the movie, *The Misfits* was in the Reno area at the time. Director John Houston offered to race a camel from the Fleishhacker Zoo (San Francisco). He did. What's more, he won.

CALLING ALL CAMELS

WHAT: International Camel and Ostrich Races

WHERE: Virginia City Arena and Fairgrounds, 458 F St., Virginia City

COST: Prices for general admission start at $15.00 and $18.00. Parking will set you back $5.00 more. The truly frugal should know that parking in Virginia City is free, and so is the shuttle that will take you to the arena.

PRO TIP: Bring a pillow to sit on—the bleachers are hard. When driving up Geiger Grade from Reno, make sure to look for wild horses. They live throughout this region and will sometimes wander onto the road.

Camel Races. Photo courtesy of Virginia City Tourism Commission.

The zany event has been a Virginia City tradition ever since. But camels—in Nevada? Bactrian camels (those with two humps) were first brought to Nevada in 1856 by the US Army. Later they were used to haul salt to the Virginia City and Austin mills. Using camels proved unsuccessful. Their feet were not tough enough for the rocky terrain, and they frightened horses and in many cases people as well. In 1875, the Nevada Legislature outlawed camels on public roadways, and this put an end to camels in Nevada. Or did it?

Decades after the last animals died or were transported elsewhere, there were sightings of ghostly camels. There's also the legend of the Red Camel ghost that wanders Mt. Davidson on moonlit nights. As far as camels on public roadways, the law was taken off the books in the 1900s.

You'll need more than a pillow if you want to become a camel jockey. Bravery and thick skin are but two. First take a $10 short walk on a camel. If you're still thick skinned and brave, they'll have you sign a waiver, give you some good tips, and—you're off.

155

PICON PUNCH AND POLTERGEISTS

What is a one-of-a-kind libation mostly known only to locals?

Although it was invented in San Francisco and is served in parts of Idaho and California, the Picon Punch cocktail is a northern Nevada tradition. Here in northern Nevada, the drink is served in a special stemmed glass rather than a highball or Collins glass used in other locales.

A drink that is an acquired taste and takes some getting used to, the Picon Punch was created by Basque immigrants in the 19th century. A caveat here, if you should order a Picon Punch in most other parts of the United States, you'd better know how to make it because the bartender probably won't.

It's not the most popular drink being served, but locals' hangouts, the Union Brewery and the Cigar and Bar, are two places in Virginia City that will make you a Picon Punch. Incidentally, both places are haunted. A fun place to hang out, the Union Brewery has a ghost that's pulled such dirty tricks he's been featured on Zak Bagans's *Ghost Adventures* TV show. Ladies, let me tell you, this ghost is a naughty one.

The Cigar and Bar is haunted by the ghost of 19th-century prostitute Julia Bulette who was murdered in her bed in 1867. There's a legend here. It's said that the undertaker who prepared

---

> If you're looking for the old biker bar that had assorted bras hanging from its chandelier, the Union Brewery is the place. The bras are gone, remodeling's been completed, and the bikers—they still love the Union.

Union Brewery

Julia's body for transport to the cemetery was such a fan that he chose to bury Bulette in a basement wall and send a rock-filled coffin to the cemetery in her stead.

The ghostly Miss Bulette is said to walk the premises on occasion. Ghost hunters will tell you this even before they've had a Picon Punch or two.

DO GHOSTS MAKE YOU THIRSTY?

WHAT: Union Brewery and the Cigar and Bar

WHERE: 63 N C St. and right next door at 69 N C St., Virginia City

COST: Cost of drinks vary.

PRO TIP: Wild horses come to town often. In accordance with nature, watch your step when treading off the boardwalk.

WORLD CHAMPIONSHIP OUTHOUSE RACES

What race requires a roll of toilet paper and a toilet seat?

With the fall thoughts turn to Halloween. Not only because it is a favorite fun night it is also Nevada Day. In Virginia City thoughts also turn to something more outlandish than grinning ghouls and jack o' lanterns—outhouse races. Frankly I'm surprised that some former Olympians haven't hastened up the hill to participate. Maybe outlandish isn't for them. Maybe all those medals weigh too heavily around their necks. Give them time. Sooner or later one of them will compete in the World Championship Outhouse Races. It is a competition. And it is opened to all. The rules are very specific for those who wish to enter their outhouse (which incidentally must be fully functional). Teams of three pushers and one rider are dressed in their most elegant attire as they roll up to compete with other fast-moving outhouses.

> **YOU'RE RACING WHAT?**
>
> **WHAT:** World Championship Outhouse Races
>
> **WHERE:** C St., Virginia City
>
> **COST:** The Outhouse race is a free event for spectators. To participate, the entry fee is $60 for each outhouse entered.
>
> **PRO TIP:** For more information, email info@liquidblueevents.com or call 775-851-4444.

Virginia City is famous for many things: the Comstock Lode, holding a parade for nearly every holiday, and colorful offbeat events such as the Rocky Mountain Oyster Fry.

Outhouse Races. Photo courtesy of Virginia City Tourism Commission.

Anticipation builds, but first things first; Virginia City is a town that never wastes an opportunity to have a parade. So, it follows that before the race can begin there will be a parade that shows off the outhouses and others held at high noon, give or take—this is Virginia City after all.

Once the parade is concluded, the races begin. This is a well-organized event. As you cheer your favorite on to victory, the question on everybody's mind is whose garishly decorated outhouse will make it to the finish line on C St. first? Like any other race, there's always a winner. Somebody will maneuver their outhouse into first place and make it across the toilet paper finish line to win the prize.

So, what you ask, is the prize. In fitting with the occasion, the prize is a golden plunger, a case of toilet paper and a monetary prize. It's all in good fun. This may be one of those events you've never heard of, but I'd be willing to bet that once you've come up to Virginia City and watched or raced an outhouse, you'll be ready to do it again next year. You may even be brave enough to compete with your own outhouse, fully functional of course.

BIGFOOT

What strange things are seen out in Six Mile Canyon?

Yes, I'm going to go there. What exactly is Bigfoot AKA Sasquatch? Does the creature even exist? A lot of people wonder about this. But more importantly, if he does exist there's the question of whether or not he, or she, actually lives in the Silver State. As someone who enjoys all the weirdly weird that Nevada offers, I'd like to think so. According to witnesses the hairy creature does indeed reside in Nevada. With the exception of downtown Las Vegas, Sasquatch, or Bigfoot if you will, has been spotted throughout the state.

One place he's been seen is outside of Virginia City, an ideal climate for Bigfoot, or so I was told by the same person who told me about seeing Bigfoot one night. Now you may be thinking that this person who saw Bigfoot near Virginia City had imbibed a little bit too much at one of the local saloons. I was ahead of you on this one, and I asked if perhaps he'd enjoyed a bit too much before the encounter. The witness however swore that this wasn't the case. He knows what he saw. And he insisted that what he saw was a big ape-like creature matching the description of Bigfoot out near Six Mile Canyon.

> The drive from Virginia City down Six Mile Canyon toward Dayton is one of the most scenic drives in the Virginia City area. As you drive down the canyon, you'll pass Sugar Loaf (east of Virginia City). It was here in Six Mile Canyon that silver ore was first discovered, giving way to early Nevada mining and the Virginia City silver boom.

View of Sugar Loaf from Virginia City

YOU NEVER KNOW WHAT YOU'LL SEE

WHAT: Site of Bigfoot sighting at Six Mile Canyon

WHERE: Somewhere between Six Mile Canyon Rd. and Hwy. 50

COST: It's free to drive the scenic road (341) from Virginia City to Dayton.

PRO TIP: If you drive the 10 miles to Dayton, be sure and check out the Dayton State Park (US Hwy. 50 and 4th Avenue) and the Dayton Cemetery at 75 Pike St., which is the oldest continually maintained cemetery in the state of Nevada.

Covered in hair and standing about eight feet tall, Bigfoot was wandering the canyon alone in the middle of the night. The witness was driving home toward Dayton when he saw the creature just off the side of the road. He stopped his car and called to Bigfoot.

Yes, I know that's not a wise thing to do, but the man wanted proof in the form of a photo that he'd indeed seen the elusive Sasquatch. Lucky for him, Sasquatch wasn't interested in having his photo posted all over Instagram and Facebook. He shrugged his mighty shoulders and took off running in the opposite direction. Without proof, we'll just have to take this man's word for it that Bigfoot lives just outside of Virginia City.

MARY JANE SIMPSON

Why is a mule buried just outside the cemetery gate?

Mary Jane Simpson's gravesite falls into the expect-the-unexpected category. And no doubt she would probably have plenty to bray about the fact that some scoundrel has stolen her monument/marker. Mary Jane was neither a gunslinger nor a lady of the evening, and she is buried there just outside the main gate of the Silver Terrace Cemetery in Virginia City.

Like so many others on the Comstock, Mary Jane earned her living in the mines and died in the great fire of 1875. So there she was, working, deep in the bowels of the earth, the morning crazy Kate Shea carelessly knocked over an oil lamp. And much like Chicago's Mother O'Leary's cow, Kate Shea started a devastating fire that destroyed most of the north side of the city. The date was October 26, 1875—the end of the line for Mary Jane. Mary Jane happened to be in the wrong place at the wrong time. By the time rescuers finally got to her, she was burned beyond recognition. One of her friends and admirers was so distraught at her untimely death that he dug a hole at the gate and buried what was left of her there. Not satisfied, he immortalized her with the following inscription that he carved on her headboard.

> Sacred to the Memory of Mary Jane Simpson
> The within was only a mule
> Still she was nobody's fool
> Stranger, tread lightly

ONLY A MULE

WHAT: Burial site of Mary Jane Simpson, the mule

WHERE: Outside the front gate of the Silver Terrace Cemetery in Virginia City

COST: Free

PRO TIP: Wear comfortable shoes, you'll want to explore this old cemetery.

Mary Jane Simpson Monument

Vandalism is a real problem at some of Nevada's old cemeteries. The monument that stands at the entrance of the Silver Terrace Cemetery in tribute to the hardworking animal has been partially destroyed. Erected by the Julia C. Bulette Chapter of the E. Clampus Vitus 90 years after her death, it has been stolen by thieves and as yet not been replaced.

According to legend, there is a glowing headstone in the cemetery that can be seen from all over town on certain nights.

LADY JUSTICE UNBLINDFOLDED

Is the courthouse rare?

With a scale in one hand and a sword in the other, Lady Justice statues are ubiquitous to courthouse buildings throughout the world. Most are blindfolded to signify that justice is blind and thus objective. In Virginia City (Storey County), the lady atop the county courthouse isn't blindfolded, and this, according to local lore, is a rarity indeed.

The Storey County Courthouse was opened in 1877, making it the oldest continuously operating county courthouse in all of Nevada. A lot of trials have taken place within these stone walls, and that's a lot of judges and a lot of juries. If the stories are true, there are a few ghosts as well. One of them is said to be Peter Larkin, who was hanged behind the courthouse about the same time it opened its doors.

Larkin might never have been convicted except that his victim appeared (in ghost form of course) to admonish his former lover and that of Larkin to tell the truth of how his death came to be. When a ghost comes calling, people tend to get nervous. This lady was no exception. She raced down to the courthouse and revised her statement, not realizing that her words would surely send Peter Larkin to the gallows. The ghost had been adamant. And she wanted a clear conscience even if it meant the death of her lover.

> Local lore has it that when notorious Mustang Ranch brothel owner Joe Conforte was an inmate in the jail here, he was kept busy by picking weeds in the area of the courthouse.

Lady Justice atop the Storey County Courthouse

JUSTICE AND GHOSTS

WHAT: Storey County Courthouse

WHERE: 26 S B St., Virginia City

COST: Free

PRO TIP: This is an operating courthouse. On days that no trials are going on, you may roam around a bit. Be sure to visit the Slammer & County Museum located inside the courthouse.

As expected, Larkin was convicted of murder and sentenced to hang. He walked to his doom through two feet of snow to the scaffold behind the courthouse on January 19, 1878. And he is not happy about that. His mournful cries can be heard throughout the courthouse at night and his ghost still walks the courthouse. He doesn't want for company. Former inmates of the old Storey County jail here inside the courthouse are also said to haunt the place.

And since she is not blindfolded, Lady Justice sees it all.

VERDI: THE GREAT TRAIN ROBBERY

Who beat Jessie James to the punch in robbing?

You meet all sorts of people during a train robbery. The West's first train robbery took place on the night of November 4, 1870, just outside of Verdi. The Central Pacific Overland Express had just left the Verdi station and was headed to Reno when the robbery occurred. One of the five bandits helping themselves to $41,600 in gold coins was a Sunday school superintendent by the name of John Chapman.

The robbers beat Jessie James to the train robbing punch by three years. James's take at $3,000 was several thousand dollars smaller as well. It didn't take long for the bandits to realize that crime doesn't pay. Chapman should have paid more attention to the Sunday school admonition Thou Shall Not Steal. He and the bunch were all captured within the week, and most of the money was reclaimed, but not all of it. This is where legend enters.

The men were convicted and sent to prison, but they had other plans. While Chapman and the others made plans for a prison break, only one of the gang desisted, Jack Davis. He remained in his cell while his compadres roamed the hills, free but hunted men. Turned out to be a wise move on Davis's part, as he was released on good behavior within three years. His pals had all been captured and their sentences extended as he rode off into the sunset—but not that far.

IT'S WHERE THE MONEY WAS

WHAT: Nevada Historical Marker 128 that marks the spot

WHERE: Bridge St. and S Verdi Rd. in Verdi

COST: Free

PRO TIP: Boomtown Hotel Casino is nearby with lots of parking, family fun center, food, and lodging.

Historic Marker at site of the Verdi Train Robbery

Legend has it that Davis held out $3,000 of the train robbery take, and that he buried his loot somewhere in Six Mile Canyon outside of Virginia City. A lot of treasure hunters have searched for Davis's cache. So far all they've encountered is the bank robber's angry ghost.

Verdi won its name fair and square. Charles Crocker, founder of the Central Pacific Railroad, named Verdi after Italian composer Giuseppe Verdi in 1868. In Nevada, however, the name Verdi is pronounced like "rib eye" and doesn't sound anything like Signor Giuseppe Verdi pronounced his name.

MARK TWAIN'S NIECE

How did Abraham Lincoln alter the course of Mark Twain's writing career?

It's a fact not generally known outside of Nevada, but humorist/writer Mark Twain played a part in Nevada's early statehood history. In 1860 newly elected President Abraham Lincoln appointed Orion Clemens to be the Nevada Territory's Secretary of State.

In order to carry out his duties as the first (and only) Secretary to the Nevada Territory, Orion left St. Louis, Missouri on July 18, 1861 accompanied by his younger brother, Samuel. When they finally arrived in Carson City, Orion was kept busy with politics. And Samuel, bored with his surroundings ventured out to try his hand at mining. When he realized that everyone who mined didn't become a millionaire, Samuel Clemens went to Virginia City, hoping to find a job.

Luck was with him. His letters to the editor caught the eye of *Territorial Enterprise* editor Joseph T. Goodman who offered him a job writing for the newspaper. Samuel Clemens had found his niche. Under the tutelage of Goodman and William Wright (Dan DeQuille) he developed his distinct writing style. His stories at the *Territorial Enterprise* were hoaxes that dealt with all manner of life and death in Virginia City: ghosts, politics, mining, social and current events.

Meanwhile down in Carson City, Orion settled in and sent for his wife and his daughter Jennie. When they arrived, the family

---

Jennie Clemens was saving money to help buy her church's first pulpit bible when she died. The women of the church donated the rest of the money to purchase the bible. Today it's on display at the church Jennie and her family attended: First Presbyterian Church, 115 N Division St., Carson City.

Jennie Clemens headstone

> ## THUS HISTORY MAY HAVE BEEN CHANGED
>
> **WHAT:** The Clemens house
>
> **WHERE:** 502 N Division St., Carson City
>
> **COST:** Although the house is privately owned, you're free to take photos and look at the house from the sidewalk. There's a bench provided at the corner for relaxing and photographing.
>
> **PRO TIP:** The colored lines on the sidewalks around this area of Carson City represent the trail of historic homes.

moved into a small house at 502 N Division St. in Carson City, a house, in which Samuel, a fun and loving uncle to Jennie, often visited. Local lore is that it was either in Carson City or Virginia City, depending on which source you believe, that Samuel Clemens took the pen name Mark Twain.

When little Jennie died of meningitis at age 9 on February 1, 1864, her parents and her uncle Samuel were devastated. After some negotiation with the local undertaker, the family buried Jennie at Lone Mountain Cemetery. Grieving deeply, Mark Twain lashed out at the undertaker two days later. In an article entitled Concerning Undertakers he claimed that the undertaker took advantage of families because he was the only undertaker in town who also owned the only cemetery in town.

Mark Twain left Nevada in May 1864. He'd challenged a man to a duel (which was against state law,) he was heartbroken and he was tired of Virginia City. Orion and his wife would never recover from the loss of their only child. They left Nevada two years later.

TRICK OR TREAT AT THE GOVERNOR'S MANSION

Why is the governor's mansion decorated for Halloween?

Halloween is a fun day across the United States. It is also a special day for Nevada. It's the date that Nevada became a state. In a twofer holiday, Nevada Day was celebrated on Halloween day (whatever day of the week it fell on) with parades, trick or treating, and closures of state business offices. Then, in 2000, someone (probably a government employee) came up with the idea that Nevada Day should be celebrated on the last Friday of October instead, thus giving state employees a three-day weekend. The Nevada legislature went to work and voila!—it was so.

The governor's mansion is tricked out in Halloween decorations for the whole month of October. Dracula, pumpkins, spiders, and other ominous-looking characters all scream the season. Yes, the governor and first lady still greet trick or treaters at the front door of the governor's mansion on October 31st. It's been a Nevada tradition since Grant Sawyer and his wife Bette resided at the mansion from 1959 to 1967.

Bring your phone and take some photos. Not every state governor celebrates Halloween. But it's fitting because the mansion is thought to be haunted by a former first lady and a ghost who hang out in a grandfather clock.

ALL GOODIES

WHAT: Trick or treat with the governor and the first lady

WHERE: Nevada Governor's Mansion, 606 Mountain St., Carson City

COST: Free

PRO TIP: The fun starts at dusk, but get there early. This is a big deal, and the crowds will be enormous. Bring a flashlight and comfortable shoes because you'll be standing in line awhile.

Nevada Governor's Mansion decorated for Halloween

The Nevada governor's mansion wasn't built until 1908 (44 years after Nevada gained statehood). Denver Dickerson became the first governor to live in the mansion when he and his family moved there in 1909. His daughter June is the only child born in the mansion as of yet. June and her mother Una are said to haunt the mansion.

ADAM UBER'S CURSE

Are curses effective?

Along Boyd Lane (now Genoa Lane) just outside Genoa there's a stand of tall cottonwood trees. Among them is a tree known as the hanging tree. It bears a plaque that tells the story of the lynching of Adam Uber on December 7, 1897. On the night Uber was lynched everyone in town probably realized what was happening, but were too frightened to speak out against the vigilantism. Two weeks earlier Uber had shot and killed Hans Anderson one of the area's favorites in a bar fight over 25 cents. Tempers flared. Anderson was dead and here was Adam Uber alive and well in their jail. Uber was facing a murder charge, but they wanted justice—now. The angry mob decided to take matters into their own hands.

They cut the telephone wires so the sheriff couldn't call for help and tricked Sheriff Brockliss and Constable Gray into opening the jailhouse door. Forcing Brockliss and Gray to come along with them, the masked men pulled the terrified Uber out of his cell, and drug the naked man down Boyd Lane toward a tall cottonwood tree. Throwing a rope around his neck, they ordered Adam Uber to say his prayers. Beyond all hope, he yelled out that he was cursing each and every one of them, and their families as well. The curse, he screamed, would follow their families for several generations.

The men howled with laughter as Adam Uber was hoisted up off his feet. When he was dead, they pulled their guns and shot at his corpse. The editor of the *Genoa Courier*, George M. Smith, was outraged, writing a strong editorial that condemned the lynching.

Although Governor Reinhold Sadler offered a $500 reward for the arrest of the men that participated in the lynching, no one was ever arrested for the crime.

Hanging Tree at Genoa

NO JUSTICE

WHAT: The Hanging Tree

WHERE: South side of Genoa Lane (halfway to Genoa off 395 S Hwy.)

COST: Free

PRO TIP: Don't turn around after seeing the tree. There is much to see and do in Nevada's oldest town of Genoa.

"Peaceful Genoa has been disgraced by its neighbors. While the poor victim . . . is perhaps better off dead than alive, there is no possible excuse for the horrible work of the lynchers. The treatment of Uber was brutal and fiendish to a terrible degree and the whole affair is a hideous disgrace to the county and the state."

But the curse proved effective. One of the mob's leaders would lose his leg in a freak accident under the same tree that Adam Uber was hanged from. One by one the men saw strange deaths and misfortune falling upon themselves and their loved ones. None of them would ever laugh at Adam Uber or his curse again.

SPIRIT CAVE MAN

Who is the oldest human mummy ever discovered in North America?

One of Nevada's most famous caves is Spirit Cave in the northern Nevada desert. The cave is on public land somewhere near the Stillwater Range, east of Fallon. Exact locations of archeological sites are protected under the Archaeological Resources Protection Act of 1979. Only certain state employees and archeologists, who hold valid state and federal antiquities permits, know where it is. This, it's hoped, will prevent further plunder and thefts of archaeological sites and burial caves in the state.

Archaeologists Sydney and Georgia Wheeler were studying the caves and rock shelters near Grimes Point when they stumbled upon the partially mummified remains of an ancient man. Known as Spirit Cave Man, it's the oldest human mummy ever discovered in North America to date.

The mummy and other artifacts from Spirit Cave were taken to the Nevada Museum in Carson City. There they were kept under lock and key until such time that they could be adequately studied. In 1996, anthropologists examined Spirit Cave Man using mass spectrometry. The findings of that test put Spirit Cave Man at about 9,400 years old. Further examination determined that Spirit Cave Man was 5'2" and that he suffered such maladies as chronic back pain, gum disease, and infections.

THERE'S HISTORY AND THEN THERE'S PREHISTORIC HISTORY

WHAT: Grimes Point

WHERE: US Hwy. 50, Fallon

COST: Free

PRO TIP: The Bureau of Land Management gives free tours of Hidden Cave on the second and fourth Saturdays of the month, except for holidays. This is your only way to see Hidden Cave.

Nevada Desert near Fallon

In the next several years, a bitter controversy swirled around Spirit Cave Man. On one side of the issue are the scientists who want to study his remains. On the other side, Native Americans don't want him studied. They claim him as their ancestor and believe he should be reburied so that he may continue his journey on to the next world. The battle moved into the federal courts. Under the 1990 Native Americans Grave Protection and Repatriation Act (NAGPRA), the tribes claimed the right to rebury Spirit Cave Man without further scientific testing. Finally, in 2016, Native Americans were given the right to rebury Spirit Cave Man . . . and his journey begins.

Indian artifacts are highly collectible and sought after. But it's against federal law for non-Native Americans to own certain artifacts, such as funeral goods and sacred objects, especially eagle feathers. If you see one, leave it be.

TORTOISE AND THE BOTTLE CAP GAZEBO

Is a City Ever too small for Art?

Fernley is 35 miles east of Reno. If you want to make a comparison to the Biggest Little City, Fernley is a small town. Small town vibe aside, this little city has a lot going on. Fernley has some big art.

Big Art for Small Towns was a joint effort launched in 2012 between the Black Rock Arts Foundation, the City of Fernley, and the Burning Man Project. Located in Fernley's new Main Street Burning Man Art Park, the resulting art work is something all can be proud of. The 25-foot-long tortoise sculpture was created by Fernley artist Pan Pantoja. The tortoise's back is covered with 4 x 4-inch ceramic tiles that were painted by Fernley students and residents with Pantoja and Reno artists Aric Shapiro and Kelsey Sweet. The tiles depict life in Fernley and Nevada.

PUBLIC ART

WHAT: Main Street Burning Man Art Park

WHERE: 610 E Main St., Fernley

COST: Free

PRO TIP: If you happen to be visiting Fernley in the spring, you don't want to miss the Fernley Fire in the Sky Lantern Festival held at the Fernley Speedway. Tickets are $50 per person on the day of the event or cheaper if bought in advance. Kids 15 and younger are free. No pets allowed.

Fernley began life as a farming and ranching community. The historic Fernley Lassen Railway Depot on Main Street was used as a railway station until 1985. It was listed on the National Register of Historic Places in 2005.

The Tortoise

Nearby is the colorful bottle cap gazebo by artists Max Poynton and Andrew Grinberg and a hundred volunteers. Created for Burning Man 2012, the gazebo is evocative of a lotus and incorporates thousands of bottle caps that have been flattened and strung together with wire to form the gazebo's leaves. This is only the beginning of the joint effort that proves no city is ever too small for art.

BLACK ROCK CITY

Is there a temporary city in Nevada?

If the idea of radical self-expression, art, and radical self-reliance interest you, this city just might be the place for you. It is offbeat and won't appeal to everyone. It certainly won't be your grandmother's idea of a place worth visiting. And there are drawbacks. The speed limit is 5 miles per hour, and no pets are allowed. Other than that, there is nothing unusual about this small city (say of nearly 70,000 people) with its own post office, airport, restaurants, police force, and emergency crews. Nothing out of the ordinary until you realize that the city is temporary and only exists for a week; such is the case of Black Rock City. The city is built on the playa in the Black Rock Desert to accommodate attendees, known as Burners, who travel from all over the world for the annual Burning Man festival. There is a jargon all its own. As an example, those Burners who come without enough resources to take care of themselves, other than their numerous amazing outfits are called Sparkle Ponies. It is expected that each Burner will bring enough supplies to see to his/her needs during the event. Sparkle Pony is not a complimentary sobriquet.

Burning Man began on Summer Solstice 1986 with the burning of an 8-foot-tall effigy on Baker Beach in San Francisco. As the

PARK YOUR ART CAR AND LOOK AROUND

WHAT: Black Rock Desert aka as BRC

WHERE: Ground zero for the Burning Man festival, Black Rock Desert

COST: Free—unless you plan on taking part in the Burning Man Festival. Tickets are in the $1,000 range.

PRO TIP: Never ever go off into the Nevada desert (or any desert for that matter) without adequate drinking water. The closest eatery is Bruno's Country Club in Gerlach.

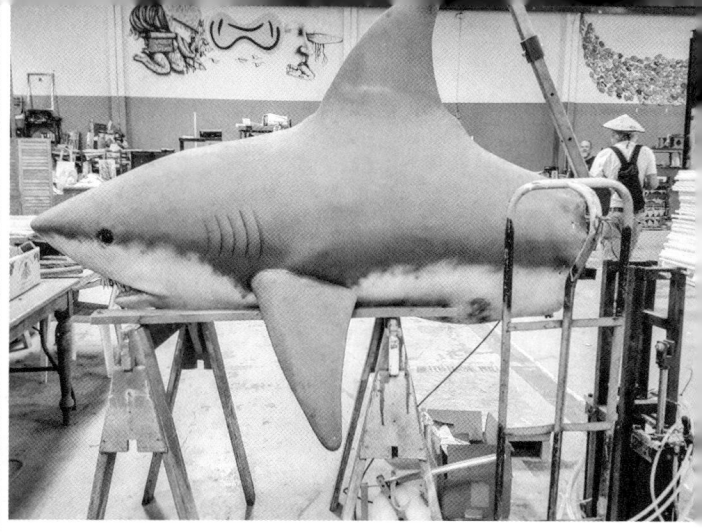

Burning Man projects in the works at the Generator where some of the art of Burning Man festival is created.

number of people wanting to participate steadily increased, the event was moved to the Black Rock Desert. Here Burning Man has grown to its current size with thousands of people participating. The event culminates each year with the burning of the man.

Burning Man is different things to different people. It is creativity, camaraderie, spirituality, art cars, outlandish costumes, art for art's sake, music, public nudity, drugs, dust, and of course, the wooden effigy of the man that is burned in a big bonfire at the end of the late summer event—an event like no other.

At the Black Rock Desert on October 15, 1997, the Thrust Supersonic car at 763 miles per hour became the first land vehicle to break the sound barrier while also breaking the land speed record.

THUNDER MOUNTAIN MONUMENT

Is there any art in the middle of the desert?

You're going to drive a little bit for this one. But trust me if you want to see something quirky, Thunder Mountain is the place. It's not your average tourist attraction, and it's located on I-80 just outside Imlay. If you're keeping track of mileage, that's about 120 miles east of Reno. Thunder Mountain is the creation of Frank Van Zant, who began his project in 1967 after having car trouble in nearby Imlay, or so the story goes. Van Zant wanted to live on this land and create his unique artwork that would show the struggles of Native Americans. So, he combed the desert, picking up the castoffs and junk of modern society. These were his media: old car parts, doll's heads, bottles, and anything else deemed worthless by those who carelessly tossed these things in the desert.

Van Zant created a three-story bottle house among his sculptures for his dwelling. There he lived, like California's Sarah Winchester of Winchester House fame, continually adding to his home and surroundings. Somewhere along the way, the World War II vet took the name Chief Rolling Mountain Thunder, claiming he was full-blooded Creek.

For the next 20 years, he worked at his art. However, art is subjective. There were those in Imlay who didn't approve of Rolling Thunder or his Thunder Mountain, even after he'd been named Nevada Artist of the Year in 1983. Arsonists struck Thunder Mountain that same year, destroying much of the site.

> There is no mountain by the name of Thunder Mountain in Nevada. Thunder Mountain Monument is on the flats not a mountain.

Thunder Mountain

ONE MAN'S ART

WHAT: Thunder Mountain (open every day from 7 a.m. to 7 p.m.)

WHERE: Take the I-80 East exit at Imlay (Exit 135). The monument is on 800 SE Star Peak Rd. (a frontage road) in Imlay.

COST: Free, but Thunder Mountain depends on donations. $2 per group is the suggested donation.

PRO TIP: The closest public restrooms and place to eat is the Star Point Trading Post and RV Park about four miles from Thunder Mountain. There's also a kiddie playground so the youngsters can romp.

Undeterred, he kept working until one day in 1989. The aged Chief Rolling Mountain Thunder wrote a hasty goodbye note and shot himself in the head. In 1992, Thunder Mountain was placed in the Nevada State Registry of Historic Places and is designated a State of Nevada Historic Site Restoration Project.

VIRGINIA CITY MALL

Did Mark Twain shop here?

No doubt this little mall would fit into Minneapolis's Mall of America thousands of times with room left over for a truckload of big-screen TVs. But hey, size isn't everything. The Virginia City Mall offers a shopping experience you won't forget. The mall has but two stores, and in those stores are at least six vendors, each with their own unique offerings.

There's a lot of junk, and there's a lot of treasures. But you know what they say about one man's trash being another's treasure. That's especially true here. Not everyone is in the market for a rusty horseshoe, a bag of old marbles, or a one-armed Barbie doll, but if you are, then you're in luck. Juxtaposition rules in this place where a vintage designer dress hangs beside a $12 Virginia City t-shirt, and a $500 ermine coat shares space with a dreary old denim jacket. Elvis and Marilyn are the king and queen of the kitschy glassware, tins, sweatshirts, handbags, and just about anything you care to name. Big-eyed Betty Boop represents alongside John Wayne sculptures. There are birdhouses, dollhouses, jewelry, cooking utensils and quilts, cameos and comic books, rare collector LPs, steins, and exquisite glassware. Name it, and chances are, you will find it here in this one-of-a-kind mall known as the Virginia City Mall.

RUMMAGING IS A SPORT

WHAT: The Virginia City Mall

WHERE: 54 N C St., Virginia City

COST: Free to take a photo in the "jail." What you spend can range from a few dollars to several hundred dollars, depending on what you buy.

PRO TIP: Don't forget to look at items on the breezeway of the mall. And while you're at it, be sure to check out the fun photo op at the jail. People come from all over the country just to get their picture taken in the little jail here at the Virginia City Mall.

The Breezeway of the Virginia City Mall

No, Mark Twain didn't shop here, but then he didn't shop at the Mall of America either. The Virginia City Mall wasn't around in Twain's time, but there is a tenuous Twain connection here. Books, and lots of them, by and about Twain can be found throughout the mall.

Mark Twain started his writing career right up the street at the *Territorial Enterprise*. The building still stands.

AT THE DRIVE-IN

Okay, but is there a snack bar?

Ever since Georges Méliès gave us the 1902 classic *A Trip to the Moon*, movie goers the world over have been hooked on the wondrous entertainment that film represents. Ours is a country that loves movies. Movie going was taken to a whole new level with drive-ins that first came into existence in the mid-1930s. Drive-ins caught on and were a big deal from the 1950s onward. The entire family could jump in the car head to the drive-in and enjoy a film in the privacy of that car. Some nights the drive-in offered the special bargain dollar a carload. Rather than pay per person the carful could go on the cheap. These weren't first run movies, but usually old black-and-white horror flicks. But who cared? The price was right.

This changed with the 1980s and the advent of VHS recorders and a vast array of video taped movies. For the first time in history a family could rent and watch first rate movies in the comfort and privacy of their own home. Imagine enjoying a meal, beyond the usual hamburgers or pizza, while watching a new movie. The public's interest was piqued with this new opportunity.

WATCH A MOVIE LIKE THEY DID IT BACK IN THE DAY

WHAT: Westwind El Rancho Drive-In

WHERE: 555 El Rancho Dr., Sparks

COST: General Admission is $8.00 per adult and $5.50 per child. Tuesday nights are family nights with reduced rates of $5.50 per adult and $2.00 per child. Call 775-358-6920 for more information.

PRO TIP: Some things never change. Just like back in the day, make sure that your windows are nice and clean to better see all the action. Be sure to bring chairs, pillows, and blankets during the summer to sit under the stars in front of your car and watch the movie. Blankets are a good idea in the cooler months for the little ones as well.

Westwind El Rancho Drive-In

On the downside, interest in drive-ins began to wane and like dominoes falling, drive-ins across the country started closing up. Today there are a little more than 300 drive-ins in the United States. Two of those are in Nevada. One is in Las Vegas and the other, the Westwind El Rancho Drive-In, is in Sparks. With four screens the drive-in can hold 550 cars.

If you haven't been to the drive-in since before VHS gave way to streaming, you might want to check out the El Rancho for some old-fashioned fun, in a 21st century way. Gone are the cumbersome hang in your window speakers and fuzzy screen images. This drive-in offers top of the line sound (your car stereo or FM equipment) and image. And yes, during intermission we can all still go to the snack bar.

On Saturdays and Sundays, the El Rancho presents a swap meet where local sellers offer fresh produce, clothes, and all types of merchandise.

NEVER ENOUGH BOOKS

Is it possible to have too many books?

Any bookworm can tell you that it is impossible to have too many books. Every book on a library shelf represents a new and different world just waiting to be discovered. The Washoe County Library in Reno offers books for every reading taste; whether it's learning a new skill, solving a cozy murder mystery, or exploring the life of a long-dead president, you'll find just the right book here.

But what if you prefer filling your own library shelf—on the cheap? This event is tailor-made for you. This is an event that you can feel good about taking part in. Not only will you find lots of bargains, but you will also be helping a worthy cause, the Friends of the Washoe County Library organization, which is a volunteer organization formed in 1980 to help raise money for the library. And we all know that when city budgets are tightened, money is allocated everywhere but to the library.

This brings us to the bi-monthly book sales that are put on for nine days at the Reno Town Mall. It is a bargain-hunting book lover's paradise. Newer and not so new books from classics

---

A WIN/WIN FOR READERS

WHAT: Friends of the Washoe County Library Book Sale

WHERE: Reno Town Mall Virginia St. and Peckham Ln.

COST: Spend as little or as much as you want. It's all for a good cause.

PRO TIP: This is a weekend event. Reno is a city that reads, so expect crowds. If you're serious about getting first dibs on the best books at the best prices, you might want to become a member of the Friends of the Washoe County Library (there are different membership tiers). The first Friday evening of the sale, members get a members-only sale and preview of the current offerings. To learn more check out their website. washoelibraryfriends.org

Reno Town Mall site of the big Friends of Washoe County Library book sale

to cookbooks are priced reasonably. But it is the $5 a bag book deal on the last Sunday of the sale that keeps readers coming back. Stop imagining a large garbage bag filled to the brim for five dollars. It's not that way. You will be given a plastic bag (or as many as you want) to fill with your favorites. Here I'll digress and confess that I once proudly stuffed 21 books into one of the bags, all for $5. Yes, the seams were close to ripping out, but what a deal!

The sale takes place right next to the Washoe County Library in Reno Town.

SOURCES

A Little Rivalry
https://www.reviewjournal.com/sports/unlv/unlv...
Haunted Reno, Janice Oberding
https://lasvegasweekly.com/as-we-see-it/2014/nov/.

General Jesse L. Reno Statue
https://www.nps.gov/people/jesse-l-reno.htm
https://historicalmarkerproject.com/markers/HM1H1O

Kiss the Courthouse Pillar
Life Magazine June 21, 1937
Haunted Reno, Janice Oberding
County Courthouses of Nevada: Temples of Justice, Ronald M. James.

Wedding Ring Bridge Legend
http://www.renohistorical.org/items/show/22
Reno Historical Society lectures
Reno Preservation Society lectures

The Biggest Little City in the World
Tough Little Town on the Truckee, John M. Townley
Tales of the Biggest Little City in the World, Patty Cafferatta
A Short History of Reno, Barbara and Myrick Land

The Blarney Stone . . . a Piece of It Anyway
http://www.brooks.casinocitytimes.com/article/kiss-the-blarney-stone-5915
www.weirdnv.com/location.php?location=521

World's Tallest Artificial Climbing Wall
http://basecampreno.com/the-big-wall
https://www.huffpost.com/entry/whitney-peak-hotel_n_5445129

Lazy Days on the Truckee
http://wildsierra.com/kayaking.htm
https://traveltips.usatoday.com/places-kayak-reno-nevada-57533.html

Jeans
www.historyofjeans.com
The History of the Invention of Blue Jeans and Denim (thoughtco.com)

The Donner Party Camped Here
The Donner Party Chronicles, Frank Mullen
https://www.kcra.com/article/winter-cannibalism..

Windy Hill (Audrey Harris Park)
https://cityseeker.com/reno/216944-windy-hill-audrey-harris-park

The Gazebo at Huffaker Mountain
https://blog.dicksonrealty.com/2019/03/reno-scenic-overlook
www.newtoreno.com/huffaker-hills-trail-reno-nevada.htm

Wa-Pai-Shone at Rose Garden idlewild Park
https://www.reno.gov/government/departments/parks..
https://virtualglobetrotting.com/map/wa-pai-shone

International Bowling Stadium, International Bowling Museum and Hall of Fame (Reno Satellite)
The National Bowling Stadium Reno | Discover Reno Tahoe (visitrenotahoe.com)

The Lear Theater
http://www.paulrwilliamsproject.org
www.leartheater.org

Artown
https://artown.org

Virginia Lake
http://visitreno.com/parks/virginia/
www.ndow.org/Bodies_Of_Water/Virginia_Lake

Giant Poker Chips
www.roadarch.com/mim/sports.html

Miss Wakayama and the Two-Headed Calf
https://www.nvhistoricalsociety.org

Giddy Up
https://www.cowboyshowcase.com/reno-rodeo-cattle-drive.html

Reno Rodeo
Reno Rodeo a History, the First 80 Years, Guy Clifton
https://renorodeo.com

An Elephant Named Bertha
Berta (Bertha), an Asian elephant at Nugget Casino, https://elephant.se/database2.php?elephant_id=1995
Bertha , The Elephant (1945–1999) - Find A Grave Memorial, https://www.findagrave.com/memorial/69772924/bertha_,-the-elephant
Nevada Nuggets: John Ascuaga's Nugget elephant Bertha (rgj.com)

Divorces and Dude Ranches
The Divorce Seekers: A Photo Memoir of a Nevada Dude Wrangler, Sandra and William McGee
http://renodivorcehistory.org/
Dempsey in Nevada, Guy Clifton

Dymaxion Car
https://automuseum.org
https://automobile.fandom.com/wiki/Dymaxion_car

The Mansion That Moved Twice
The Lake Mansion Home to Reno's Founding Families, Patty Cafferatta
www.renohistorical.org/items/show/34
https://www.artsforallnevada.org/rent-the-mansion/tours

Reno's Greatest Unsolved Mystery
www.renohistorical.org/items/show/47
Haunted Reno, Janice Oberding
https://backyardtraveler.blogspot.com/2008/03/mystery-of-roy-frisch.html

Marilyn's Last Film
Haunted Reno, Janice Oberding
https://silverscreenings.org/2018/04/26/the-last
https://www.backstage.com/magazine/article/nevada

The Prospector at the Chocolate Nugget Candy Factory
https://chocolatenuggetcandyfactory.com

Reno's Genie
http://www.weirdnv.com/location.php?location=830

The Brüka Theatre
www.bruka.org

Believe in Burning Man Art
https://burningman.org

The Eddy
https://theeddyreno.com

Galena Creek Bridge
https://www.onlyinyourstate.com/nevada/remarkable-bridge-nv

Orson Hyde's Curse
http://nevadaweb.com/nevadaca/curse.html
https://www.tahoetopia.com/news/curse-orson-hyde

Steamboat Hot Springs
https://steamboatsprings.org
http://twainquotes.com/18630825t.html
Dempsey in Nevada, Guy Clifton

Pyramid Lake Water Babies
Weird Las Vegas and Nevada, Joe Oesterle and Tim Cridland
Haunted Nevada Ghosts and Strange Phenomena of the Silver State, Janice Oberding
https://www.onlyinyourstate.com/nevada/pyramid-lake-legends-ny

Judas Priest: Subliminal Message Trial
https://www.greenandblackmusic.com/home/2018/10/11/judas...
https://www.blabbermouth.net/news/how-judas-priest..

Lincoln Highway Bridge Rails
https://lincolnhighwayassoc.org/info/nv
www.waymarking.com/waymarks/WMJ57B_The_Lincoln...

Pyramid Lake: Two Legends and a Fish
https://www.onlyinyourstate.com/nevada/pyramid-lake-legends-ny

That Terrible Thanksgiving
Infamous Reno, Janice Oberding
https://carsonnow.org/story/07/13/2019/nevada-lore

Lynched for a Murder That Didn't Happen
Tough Little Town on the Truckee, John M. Townley
Haunted Reno, Janice Oberding

Harolds Club Wagon Trail Mural
Reno's Big Gamble, Alicia Barber
Dateline Reno, Don Dondero
The Rise of the Biggest Little City, Dwayne Kling
https://onlinenevada.org/articles/harolds-club-mural

Oxbow Nature Study Area
www.ndow.org/.../Oxbow_Nature_Study_Area

The Depot
https://thedepotreno.com

Play Ball . . . Bocce Ball
https://bundoxbocce.com/

The Silver Dollar Scandal
The Curious Life of Nevada's LaVere Redfield: the Silver Dollar King, Jack Harpster
http://www.renocoinclub.org/redfield.html

Shamrocks for Bill Blanchfield
Infamous Reno, Janice Oberding
https://www.findagrave.com/memorial/101406777/william-f.-blanchfield
https://www.irishnevada.org/events/event/celtic-community...

Street Vibrations Motorcycle Spring and Fall Rally
https://www.streetvibrations.com
https://www.visitrenotahoe.com/featured-events/street-vibrations

Zebras, Tigers, and Shrunken Heads . . . Oh My!
https://washoecounty.us/parks/maycenterhome/index.php
https://www.washoecounty.us/parks/parks_and_trails/
https://www.expedia.com/Rancho-San-Rafael-Park..

Lucky Lindy Lands in Reno on September 19, 1927
https://www.kunr.org/post/when-lucky-lindy-came-reno
http://sparksmuseum.org/nevada-aviation-history

Take Him Home Tonight
https://nevadafilm.com/scene-in-nevada-take-me-home-tonight/
https://www.last.fm/music/Eddie+Money/_/Take+Me+Home+Tonight

Ducks in a Row
https://www.duckrace.com/reno
www.newtoreno.com/duck-race-festival-reno-nevada.htm

Silver Baron's Silver Tea Set
https://elkodaily.com/stories-of-old-nevada-the
https://www.unr.edu/mackay/keck-museum/mackay-silver
https://www.spencermarks.com/blogs/journal/the..

At the Quad
https://www.unr.edu/arboretum/areas-of-interest/historic-quadrangle
www.renohistorical.org/items/show/75
https://www.unr.edu/arboretum

James D. Hoff Peace Officer Memorial
www.hoffmemorial.org
www.findagrave.com/memorial/128550767/james-duane-hoff

Let the Games Begin
www.rgj.com/story/sports/2014/02/08/checkers-world-record-set-in-reno/5322
https://www.guinnessworldrecords.com/world-records/.

Atlas Isn't Shrugging
https://www.europeanfitnesscenter.com

Shine On, Reno Star
www.waymarking.com/waymarks/WMJQA2_The_Reno_Star_Reno_NV
www.renogatewayproject.com/reno-playa-art-park

Midtown District: A Bohemian Vibe
https://www.renomidtowndistrict.com/shopping
www.junkeeclothingexchange.com

The Count and the Countess
https://www.tmcc.edu/news/2019/10/tmcc-tales..
https://www.newsreview.com/reno/content/the-year-in-review/21575
https://local.yahoo.com/info-224848767-countess-angela-dandini-gardens-reno

The Galveston Giant Trounces the Great White Hope
https://www.americanhistoryusa.com/jack-johnson.
https://www.sutori.com/story/the-galveston-giant
Johnson-Jefferies: Dateline Reno: The Fight of the Century, Ray Hagar and Guy Clifton

Skyjacker
https://www.history.com/news/who-was-d-b-cooper
https://www.rgj.com/story/news/2014/11/24/reno

Sparks Marina Park
www.ndow.org/Bodies_Of_Water/Sparks_Marina_Park_Pond/
https://www.kunr.org/post/sparks-marina-past-present-future

Scheels Ferris Wheel, Aquarium, and Arcade
The Man Who Invented the Ferris Wheel; the Genius of George Ferris, Dani Sneed
www.scheels.com
https://www.scheels.com/stores/nevada/reno-sparks/..

Bat Bridge (McCarran Bridge)
https://www.onlyinyourstate.com/nevada/bat-bridge-nv/
https://www.kolotv.com/2020/09/06/watch-bats-fly-out-to-feed-at-night-in-sparks

The Volkswagen Bug
https://www.rgj.com/story/news/2015/04/22/reno.
https://weburbanist.com/2011/08/07/spider-bug-15.

Last Chance Joe
https://sparksmuseum.org/exhibits/last-chance-joe
www.39northdowntown.com/last-chance-joe

Camel and Ostrich Races
Camels in Nevada, Douglas McDonald,
https://visitvirginiacitynv.com/events/international-camel-ostrich-race

Picon Punch and Poltergeists
Conversation with Dawn Grant
World Championship Outhouse Races
https://visitvirginiacitynv.com/events/world-championship-outhouse-races

Bigfoot
2017 Interview

Mary Jane Simpson
https://www.nevadaappeal.com/news/local/the-saga-of-mary-jane-simpson
www.juliacbulette.com/blog/historical-plaques

Lady Justice Unblindfolded
https://storeycounty.org/202/Courthouse
https://www.nps.gov/nr/travel/nevada/sto.htm
https://www.onlyinyourstate.com/nevada/haunted-virginia-city-nv

Verdi: The Great Train Robbery
https://noehill.com/nv_washoe/nev0128.asp
https://nevadamagazine.com/issue/march-april-2018/5504
https://www.nevadaappeal.com/news/lahontan-valley/...

Mark Twain's Niece
www.twainquotes.com/jennie.html
Cemeteries of Carson City and Carson Valley, Cindy Southerland

Trick or Treat at the Governor's Mansion
100 Years in the Governor's Mansion, Jack Harpster
Haunted Nevada Ghosts and Strange Phenomena of the Silver State, Janice Oberding
https://blog.diamondresorts.com/hunt-for-tricks-and-treats-in-lake-tahoe-this-halloween

Adam Uber's Curse
https://epubs.nsla.nv.gov/statepubs/epubs/210777-1973-1Spring.pdf
Haunted Nevada Ghosts and Strange Phenomena of the Silver State, Janice Oberding

Spirit Cave Man
https://onlinenevada.org/articles/spirit-man-overview
https://www.mysterywire.com/mysteries/born-more..
https://allaroundnevada.com/spirit-cave

Tortoise and the Bottle Cap Gazebo
https://travelnevada.com/arts-culture/main-street-art-park
https://burningman.org/culture/civic-initiatives/big-art-for-small-towns
https://maps.roadtrippers.com/us/fernley-nv/points

Black Rock City
https://wikitravel.org/en/black_rock_city
https://burningman.org

Thunder Mountain Monument
http://www.thundermountainmonument.com
https://travelnevada.com/indian-culture/thunder-mountain-monument/

Virginia City Mall
https://visitvirginiacitynv.com/antiques

At the Drive-In
Drive-In Theaters; A History from Their Inception in 1933, Kenny Segrave
https://www.driveinmovie.com/history-of-drive-ins
https://www.westwinddi.com/locations/el-rancho

Never Enough Books
https://wwwwashoelibraryfriends.org

INDEX

Aquarium, 94, 146–147
Artown, 11, 30–33
Atlas, 132–133
Bagans, Zak, 156
Bat Bridge, 148–149
Bigfoot, 160–161
Blanchfield, Bill, 112–113
Blarney Stone, 1, 12–13
Bowling, 28–29
Brüka Theatre, 60–61, 63
Bulette, Julia, 156
Burning Man, 34, 52, 62–63, 103, 107, 134–136, 178–179,
Camel and Ostrich Races, 154–155
Cannibals, 20
Carson City, 3, 66–67, 114, 146, 168-169, 170, 174
Cattle Drive, 40–41
Chase, John Paul, 52
Checkers, 130–131
Chief Rolling Mountain Thunder, 180–181
Cigar and Bar, 156–157
Civilian Conservation Corps, 34
Clemens, Jennie, 168–169
Clemens, Orion, 168
Countess Angelina Dandini Garden, 138–139
Crumley, Newt, 108
Davis, Jacob, 18–19
DeLongchamps, Frederic, 106
Dempsey, Jack, 46, 70, 84
DeQuille, Dan, 168
di Cessena, Count Alexandro Dandini, 138
Divorce, 1, 6, 8–10, 46–47, 50, 54, 138
Donner Party, 20–21
Duck Race, 122–123
Elko, 108, 112, 126
Fallon, 174–175
Fernley, 176
Ferrel, C.P., 140

Ferris wheel, 94, 146–147
Ford, Priscilla, 80–81
Fremont, John C., 2–3, 16, 73
Fremont Cannon, 2–3
Friends of the Washoe County Library, 186
Friendship Doll, 38–39
Frisch, Roy, 52–53
Gable, Clark, 1, 54
Galena Creek Bridge, 66–67
Ghost, 1, 21, 50–51, 54, 61, 65, 70, 82, 155–157, 164–165, 167–168, 170
Grimes Point, 174
Guinness World Record, 130
Gutzom Borglum, 126
Harolds Club, 84–85
Hillside Cemetery, 112–113
Hoff, James D., 128–129
Huffaker Mountain Trail, 24–25
Hyde, Orson, 68–69
Idlewild Park, 26–27, 128
Imlay, 180–181
Johnson, Jack, 140–141
Japan, 38–39
Jeans, 18–19, 46, 147
Jefferson, Thomas, 127
Jeffries, Jim 140
Judas Priest, 74–75
Kayaking, 17
Lake Mansion, 50–51, 53
Larkin, Peter, 164–165
Last Chance Joe, 151–153
Lawlor Events Center, 120–121
Lear Theater, 30–31
Legends Mall, 145–146
Levi Strauss Co., 18–19
Lincoln, Abraham, 1, 168
Lindberg, Charles, 118
London, Jack, 140–141
Lone Mountain Cemetery, 169
MacKay, John, 124–126

May, Wilbur D., 116
McCarran Bridge, 148
Midtown, 136–137
Miller, Arthur, 1, 47, 54
Misfits, The, 1, 7-8, 54, 154
Miss Wakayama, 38
Money, Eddie, 120–121
Monroe, Marilyn, 1, 7–8, 47, 54–55
Motorcycle, 114–115, 129
Mount Rushmore, 1, 126
Myron Lake, 50, 74
Nelson, Baby Face, 52
Nevada Governor's Mansion, 138, 170–171
Ortiz, Luis, 82,
Outhouse Races, 1, 158–159
Oxbow Nature Study, 104–105
Paiute Legend, 78
Picon Punch, 1, 97, 156–157
Pioneer Center for the Performing Arts, 4–5, 49
Poltergeist, 97, 156
Powning Park, 4, 119
Pyramid Lake, 16, 47, 55, 72–73, 78–79
Rancho San Rafael Regional Park, 116–117
Rattlesnake Mountain, 20–21
Redfield, LaVere, 110
Reno, General Jesse L., 4
Reno Livestock Events Center, 43
Reno Riverwalk, 52
Reno Rodeo, 40–44
Reno Star, 134–135
Riverside Artist Lofts, 46–47, 65
Roberts, E.E., 10, 119
Rose Garden, 26–27, 128
Rover, J.W., 65

Silver Terrace Cemetery, 162–163
Simpson, Mary Jane, 162–163
Skyjacker, 142
Slide Mountain, 25, 68–69
Sparks, 30, 50, 56, 84–85, 144–146, 148, 150–153, 184–185
Sparks Marina Park, 96, 144–145
Sparks Museum and Cultural Center, 153
Spector, Ronnie, 121
Spirit Cave Man, 174–175
St. Patrick's Day, 12, 113
Thanksgiving, 80, 142
Train Robbery, 166–167
Twain, Mark, 1, 70–71, 154, 168–169, 182–183
Two-Headed Calf, 38–39
Uber, Adam, 90, 172–173
Union Brewery, 156–157
University of Nevada Las Vegas, 2
University of Nevada Reno, 1, 2, 112, 121, 124–126, 138
Van Tilburg Clark, Walter, 104
Van Zant, Frank, 180
Verdi, 77, 166–167
Virginia City, 18, 70, 104, 114–115, 124, 126, 129, 154–162, 164–165, 167–169, 182–183
Virginia City Mall, 182–183
Virginia Lake, 34–35, 99, 110
Wa-Pai-Shone, 26–27
Wedding Ring Bridge, 8, 55, 83, 88
Westwind El Rancho Drive-in, 184–185
Williams, Paul Revere, 30–31
Windy Hill, 22–23
Wingfield Park, 16, 32–33, 122
Wolf Pack Basketball, 121